ACE YOUR EXERCISE AND NUTRITION SCIENCE PROJECT

Titles in the
ACE YOUR BIOLOGY SCIENCE PROJECT series:

Ace Your Animal Science Project:
Great Science Fair Ideas

ISBN-13: 978-0-7660-3220-0
ISBN-10:   0-7660-3220-5

Ace Your Exercise and Nutrition
Science Project:
Great Science Fair Ideas

ISBN-13: 978-0-7660-3218-7
ISBN-10:   0-7660-3218-3

Ace Your Human Biology
Science Project:
Great Science Fair Ideas

ISBN-13: 978-0-7660-3219-4
ISBN-10:   0-7660-3219-1

Ace Your Plant Science Project:
Great Science Fair Ideas

ISBN-13: 978-0-7660-3221-7
ISBN-10:   0-7660-3221-3

Ace Your Science Project
About the Senses:
Great Science Fair Ideas

ISBN-13: 978-0-7660-3217-0
ISBN-10:   0-7660-3217-5

ACE YOUR BIOLOGY SCIENCE PROJECT

ACE YOUR EXERCISE AND NUTRITION SCIENCE PROJECT

Robert Gardner
Barbara Gardner Conklin
Salvatore Tocci

GREAT SCIENCE FAIR IDEAS

 Enslow Publishers, Inc.
40 Industrial Road
Box 398
Berkeley Heights, NJ 07922
USA

http://www.enslow.com

Library of Congress Cataloging-in-Publication Data

Gardner, Robert, 1929–
  Ace your exercise and nutrition science project: great science fair ideas / Robert Gardner, Barbara Gardner Conklin, and Salvatore Tocci.
      p. cm. — (Ace your biology science project)
  Includes bibliographical references and index.
  Summary: "Presents several science projects and science project ideas about exercise and nutrition"—Provided by publisher.
  ISBN-13: 978-0-7660-3218-7
  ISBN-10: 0-7660-3218-3
  1. Exercise–Physiological aspects–Experiments–Juvenile literature. 2. Nutritional Experiments–Juvenile literature. 3. Science projects–Juvenile literature. 4. Science fairs–Juvenile literature. I. Conklin, Barbara Gardner. II. Tocci, Salvatore. III. Title.
  QP301.G368 2010
  612.7'6—dc22   2008030798

Printed in the United States of America
102010 Lake Book Manufacturing, Inc., Melrose Park, IL

10 9 8 7 6 5 4 3 2

To Our Readers: We have done our best to make sure all Internet Addresses in this book were active and appropriate when we went to press. However, the author and the publisher have no control over and assume no liability for the material available on those Internet sites or on other Web sites they may link to. Any comments or suggestions can be sent by e-mail to comments@enslow.com or to the address on the back cover.

♻ Enslow Publishers, Inc., is committed to printing our books on recycled paper. The paper in every book contains 10% to 30% post-consumer waste (PCW). The cover board on the outside of each book contains 100% PCW. Our goal is to do our part to help young people and the environment too!

The experiments in this book are a collection of the authors' best experiments, which were previously published by Enslow Publishers, Inc. in *Health Science Projects About Nutrition, Health Science Projects About Sports Performance, Science Fair Success Using Household Products,* and *Science Fair Success Using Supermarket Products.*

Illustration Credits: Stephen F. Delisle, Figures 1, 3, 4, 5, 6, 7, 8, 9, 13, 14, 15, 19, 21; Gary Koellhoffer, Figures 17, 18, 20, 22; Enslow Publishers, Inc., Figures 11, 12, 16; LifeART image copyright 1988 Lippincott Williams & Wilkins. All rights reserved, Figure 2; USDA, Figure 10.

Photo Credits: © bubaone/iStockphoto.com, trophy icons; Centers for Disease Control and Prevention, pp. 75, 77;© Chen Fu Soh/iStockphoto.com, backgrounds; Shutterstock, pp. 1, 3, 12; United States Department of Agriculture, p. 56.

Cover Photos: Shutterstock

CONTENTS

◐ *Indicates experiments that offer ideas for science fair projects.*

Indicates experiments that offer ideas for science fair projects.

INTRODUCTION

When you hear the word *science*, do you think of a person in a white lab coat surrounded by beakers of bubbling liquids, specialized lab equipment, and computers? What exactly is science? Maybe you think science is only a subject you learn in school. Science is much more than that.

Science is the study of the things that are all around you, every day. No matter where you are or what you are doing, scientific principles are at work. You don't need special materials or equipment—or even a white lab coat—to be a scientist. Materials commonly found in your home, at school, or at a local store will allow you to become a scientist and pursue an area of interest. By making careful observations and asking questions about how things work, you can begin to design experiments to investigate a variety of questions. You can do science. You probably already have but just didn't know it!

Perhaps you are reading this book because you are looking for an idea for a science fair project for school, or maybe you are just hoping to find something fun to do on a rainy day. This book will provide an opportunity for you to learn about exercise and nutrition and how they affect your health. You will measure your heart rate, breathing rate, blood pressure, and temperature and investigate how they are affected by body position, exercise, and conditioning. You will then have an opportunity to evaluate your metabolic needs, design a diet to meet them, and explore healthy eating habits. Finally, you may choose to conduct experiments involving products that promote good health and hygiene.

SCIENCE FAIRS

Many of the experiments in this book may be appropriate for science fair projects. Experiments marked with a symbol (🔾) include a section called Science Fair Project Ideas. The ideas in this section provide suggestions to help you develop your own original science fair project. However, judges at such fairs do not reward projects or experiments that are simply copied from a book. For example, a picture of a food pyramid, which is commonly found at these fairs, would probably not impress judges unless it was done in a novel or creative way. On the other hand, a carefully performed experiment to determine the amount of energy in different snack foods would probably receive careful consideration.

Science fair judges tend to reward creative thought and imagination. However, it's difficult to be creative or imaginative unless you are really interested in your project. If you decide to do a project, be sure to choose a topic that appeals to you. Consider, too, your own ability and the cost of materials. Don't pursue a project that you can't afford.

If you decide to use a project found in this book for a science fair, you will need to find ways to modify or extend it. That should not be difficult because you will probably find that as you do these projects new ideas for experiments will come to mind. These new experiments could make excellent science fair projects, particularly because they spring from your own mind and are interesting to you.

If you decide to enter a science fair and have never done so before, you should read some of the books listed in the Further Reading section. The books that deal specifically with science fairs will provide plenty of helpful hints and lots of useful information that will enable you to avoid the pitfalls that sometimes plague first-time entrants. You will learn how to prepare appealing reports that include charts and graphs, how to set up and display your work, how to present your project, and how to relate to judges and visitors.

SAFETY FIRST

As with many activities, safety is important in science, and certain rules apply when conducting experiments. Some of the rules below may seem obvious to you, but each is important to follow.

- Have **an adult** help you whenever the book advises.

- Wear eye protection and closed-toe shoes (rather than sandals) and tie back long hair.

- Don't eat or drink while doing experiments and never taste substances being used.

- Avoid touching chemicals.

- When doing these experiments, use only nonmercury thermometers, such as those filled with alcohol. The liquid in some thermometers is mercury. It is dangerous to breathe mercury vapor. If you have mercury thermometers, ask an adult to take them to a local mercury thermometer exchange location.

- Do only those experiments that are described in the book or those that have been approved by **an adult**.

- Never engage in horseplay or play practical jokes.

- Before beginning, read through the entire experimental procedure to make sure you understand all instructions. Clear extra items from your work space.

- At the end of every activity, clean all materials and put them away. Wash your hands thoroughly with soap and water.

THE SCIENTIFIC METHOD

All scientists look at the world and try to understand how things work. They make careful observations and conduct research about a question. Different areas of science use different approaches. Depending on the phenomenon being investigated, one method is likely to be more appropriate than another. Designing a new medication for heart disease, studying the spread of an invasive plant species such as purple loosestrife, and finding evidence about whether there was once water on Mars all require different methods.

Despite the differences, however, all scientists use a similar general approach to do experiments. It is called the scientific method. In most experiments, some or all of the following steps are used: making an observation, formulating a question, making a hypothesis (an answer to the question) and prediction (an if-then statement), designing and conducting an experiment, analyzing results and drawing conclusions, and accepting or rejecting the hypothesis. Scientists then share their findings with others by writing articles that are published in journals. After—and only after—a hypothesis has repeatedly been supported by experiments can it be considered a theory.

You might be wondering how to get an experiment started. When you observe something in the world, you may become curious and think of a question. Your question can be answered by a well-designed investigation. Your question may also arise from an earlier experiment or from background reading. Once you have a question, you should make a hypothesis. Your hypothesis is a possible answer to the question (what you think will happen). Once you have a hypothesis, it is time to design an experiment.

In some cases, it is appropriate to do a controlled experiment. This means there are two groups treated exactly the same except for the single factor that you are testing. That factor is often called a variable. For example, if you want to investigate whether exercise affects heart rate, two groups may be used. One group is called the control group, and the other is called the experimental group. The two groups of people should be treated exactly the same. The people in the control group will sit quietly for five minutes while the people in the experimental group will jog in place for five minutes. The variable is exercise—it is the thing that changes, and it is the only difference between the two groups.

During the experiment, you will collect data. For example, you will measure heart rate after the period of five minutes of either rest or exercise. You might also note how quickly each person is breathing and the color of each person's face. By comparing the data collected from the control group with the data collected from the experimental group, you will draw conclusions. Since the two groups were treated exactly alike except for exercising, an increase in heart rate of the people in the experimental group would allow you to conclude with confidence that increased heart rate is a result of the one thing that was different: exercise.

Two other terms that are often used in scientific experiments are *dependent* and *independent* variables. One dependent variable here is heart rate, because it is the one you measure as an outcome. It may depend upon exercise. Exercise is the independent variable; it is the one you change on purpose. After the data is collected, it is analyzed to see whether the hypothesis was supported or rejected. Often, the results of one experiment will lead you to a related question, or they may send you off in a different direction. Whatever the results, there is something to be learned from all scientific experiments.

Chapter 1

Defining and Assessing Good Health

HUMANS HAVE ALWAYS BEEN ACTIVE. Our prehistoric ancestors were always in search of food; they had to fight other predators for sustenance or flee to safety. Our colonial ancestors also led active lives in order to survive. Physical work was a major part of the daily lives of farmers and pioneers in early America.

Automation and technology have lessened the need for physical labor. Although exercise is no longer an essential part of most of our lives, we need regular exercise to stay healthy. We no longer have to flee from woolly mammoths or fight for food, but our bodies still possess the "fight or flight" response. The stress we deal with is different from that of our ancestors, but the response to stress is the same. When we sense stress, the brain puts the body on full alert. There is an increased production of the stress-related hormones adrenaline and cortisol. In response to these hormones the heart beats faster, blood pressure rises, muscles become tense, and the body produces chemicals that are natural pain deflectors and performance enhancers. The pupils of the eyes dilate and hearing becomes more acute. The body is prepared for action—to fight or take flight.

If the stress does not require physical action, which is very often the case in modern society, our bodies are not relieved of the stress. Constant tension can make the muscles sore and rigid. Tight neck and shoulder muscles can make the head throb. Stomach acid secreted in response to stress can cause heartburn, cramps, and other digestive disorders. Instead of being "washed away" by physical activity, the chemicals released in the "fight or flight" response can accumulate in our bodies and interfere with our ability to fight infections. Other physical responses to stress include high blood pressure, fatigue, and insomnia. Our bodies need physical activity to relieve stress and maintain health. If your lifestyle does not include regular physical activity, then you need an exercise program.

Exercise, such as walking, jumping, running, and playing sports, requires energy. Our bodies also need many different substances to maintain and grow tissues such as skin, bone, muscle, hair, and nails. The energy comes from the food we eat. For good health and to keep our bodies in working order, we need a regular supply of water and nutritious food. A balanced diet provides just the right amount of energy to fuel and maintain a healthy body.

Several body systems cooperate to provide our bodies with energy and movement. The digestive system turns the food we eat into the fuel we need for energy. Our respiratory system provides oxygen to release energy from the fuel. Our circulatory system carries the fuel and oxygen to all parts of our bodies. Our urinary, excretory, and respiratory systems remove waste materials from our bodies. Our skeletal and muscular systems provide support and allow our bodies to move. The nervous system carries the impulses from the brain and spinal cord that cause muscles to contract.

No system in the human body works in isolation. Each system aids—and is aided by—all the others. When all these systems are in good working order, the body is healthy.

What is the definition of a healthy person? Some people might use physical features to describe a healthy person. Such terms might include "muscular" or "lean," but physical features are only part of good health. Good health requires a body that is strong enough to allow the person to perform daily tasks and to enjoy leisure activities, such as sports. There are four basic components of physical fitness that relate directly to a healthy body. They are cardiorespiratory fitness (a strong heart and lungs), flexibility, muscular strength and endurance, and body composition.

There are many advantages to being physically fit and healthy. These advantages include a lower risk of life-threatening heart disease or high blood pressure. In daily life physically fit people have better weight control, increased energy, and greater body flexibility and strength, meaning less chance of injury. They also often discover they have more self-confidence, clearer thinking, and a calmer response to stressful events.

SOME NECESSARY TOOLS AND SKILLS

Some experiments presented in this chapter require the use of some common medical instruments. The instruments, which are not expensive, may be available in your home or at your school's science or medical department.

The following experiments are designed to help you learn how to use the instruments and develop the skills needed to measure heart rate, breathing rate, body temperature, and blood pressure. Doctors and nurses call these measurements the "vital signs." Learning these skills will enable you to carry out experiments to find out how exercise and physical conditioning affect the vital signs.

Materials:

- a volunteer
- stopwatch, or clock or watch with a second hand
- stethoscope

Usually you can't feel your heart beat. After vigorous exercise, or if you are scared, you can feel it. You can, however, always determine your heart rate by taking your pulse.

Each time your heart beats it forces blood into your arteries. The added blood swells the elastic walls of the large arteries near your heart, sending a pulse of expansion along the walls of those arteries. It is much like the movement of a wave along a rope or Slinky. The expansion of the radial artery, on the underside of the wrist, can be felt every time the heart beats. It is where doctors and nurses take your pulse. To feel a pulse, place your two middle fingers on the inside of your own or a volunteer's wrist, as shown in Figure 1. Can you feel the pulse?

[FIGURE 1]

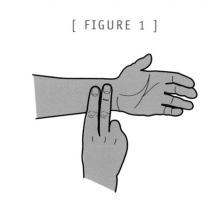

To take a pulse, place your middle finger and index finger on the underside of the subject's wrist, just behind the thumb, as shown.

Now that you know how to take a pulse, use a stopwatch, or clock or watch with a second hand to measure your heart rate (number of beats per minute). Count the number of heartbeats over a thirty-second period when you are resting comfortably. Multiply this number by two to obtain your resting heart rate in beats per minute. What is your resting heart rate? What is the resting heart rate of your volunteer? What are the resting heart rates of the people in your family?

A pulse can be felt on any artery that is close to the body's surface. For example, you can feel the pulsing of the carotid arteries on either side of your neck below the jawbone and just forward from your ear. You can also feel (and sometimes see) the pulse of the temporal artery just in front of your ear. In what other places on your body can you find a pulse? If you find a pulse at a point on the left side of your body, can you always find a pulse on the corresponding point on the right side?

If you take your volunteer's pulse at both the neck and the wrist at the same time, which pulse do you expect to feel first? Try it! Were you right?

MEASURING HEART RATE WITH A STETHOSCOPE

To hear how each throb of a pulse is caused by a contracting heart, use a stethoscope to listen to your volunteer's heart while taking his or her pulse. Place the stethoscope's ear tips in your ears and the chest piece slightly to the left of the center of the person's chest. Move the chest piece slightly until you hear the heart sounds clearly. Listen for two sounds in close succession. The first is a relatively long, booming sound. The second is a short, sharp sound. Together they make a "lubb-dup" sound. The "lubb" is caused by the contracting muscle and the closing of the valves between the heart's chambers (the ventricles and atria). The "dup" is the sound made by the closing of the valves between the heart and the two major arteries into which blood is pumped (the aorta and the pulmonary artery). These arteries and valves can be seen in the diagram of the heart shown in Figure 2.

If you don't have a stethoscope, you can hear heart sounds by placing your ear against your volunteer's chest.

Where would you place the chest piece of a stethoscope to hear blood flowing through a person's carotid arteries? Can you hear the blood flowing through these arteries that lead to the head?

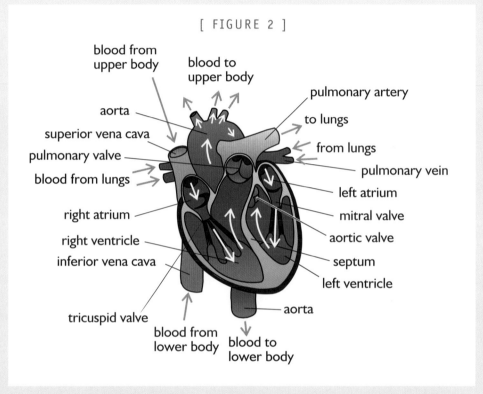

[FIGURE 2]

blood from upper body

blood to upper body

pulmonary artery

aorta

to lungs

superior vena cava

from lungs

pulmonary valve

pulmonary vein

blood from lungs

left atrium

right atrium

mitral valve

right ventricle

aortic valve

inferior vena cava

septum

left ventricle

tricuspid valve

aorta

blood from lower body

blood to lower body

A schematic drawing of the heart shows its four chambers. They consist of the right and left atria and the right and left ventricles. The diagram also shows the main veins carrying blood to the heart—the superior and inferior vena cava and the pulmonary veins—as well as the two main arteries carrying blood from the heart—the aorta and the pulmonary artery. Shown, too, are the aortic valve, the pulmonary valve, and the valves between the auricles and ventricles—the tricuspid valve and the mitral valve.

1.2 What Is Your Breathing Rate?

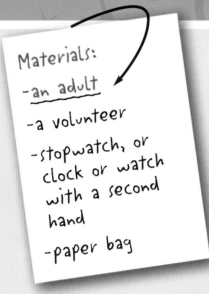

Materials:

- an adult
- a volunteer
- stopwatch, or clock or watch with a second hand
- paper bag

Have your volunteer lie on his or her back on a couch or floor. Watch your volunteer's chest move up slightly with each inhalation. Using a stopwatch, or clock with a second hand, determine how many times the person breathes in one minute. What is the person's breathing rate? What is your breathing rate? How can you measure the breathing rate if your volunteer is standing?

Can you think of another way to measure your volunteer's breathing rate?

As you probably know, some of the oxygen in the air you inhale is transferred from your lungs to your blood. At the same time, some of the carbon dioxide in your blood passes into the air in your lungs. As a result of this exchange of gases, exhaled air has less oxygen and more carbon dioxide than inhaled air.

What do you predict will happen to your breathing rate and depth of breathing if you breathe the same air over and over again? Under adult supervision, you can find out by placing the open end of a paper bag tightly around your nose and mouth. Breathe and rebreathe the air in the bag for a minute or two. What happens to your breathing rate? What happens to your depth of breathing (the volume of air you take into your lungs with each breath)? How can you explain the changes in breathing you observe?

1.3 What Is Your Blood Pressure?

Materials:

-an adult

-a volunteer

-an instrument to measure blood pressure

Pressure is defined as force per area (force ÷ area). The pressure you exert on the floor is your weight divided by the area of your shoes touching the floor. Blood pressure is the force that blood exerts against the surface area of blood vessel walls. Blood pressure in arteries is greatest when the heart is contracting, forcing more blood into these vessels. It is lowest when the heart is between pumps.

Blood pressure involves two measurements: systolic pressure and diastolic pressure. Systolic pressure is the larger one. It occurs when the heart contracts, pushing blood into the arteries. Diastolic pressure appears just before the heart contracts, when the pressure in the arteries is at a minimum.

The systolic pressure is recorded first, followed by the diastolic pressure. A normal record of blood pressure might read 120/70. The pressures are measured in millimeters (mm) of mercury. The pressure of Earth's atmosphere at sea level, which we measure with a barometer, is normally 760 mm of mercury. That means the air can support a column of mercury 760 mm high, which is the same pressure as 10.1 newtons per square centimeter, or 14.7 pounds per square inch. Of course, blood, like the rest of your body, is subject to air pressure. Consequently, blood pressure is the pressure by which the blood's pressure in arteries exceeds that of the air.

Pulse pressure is the difference between systolic and diastolic blood pressure. In the example given above, the pulse pressure would be

$$120 - 70 = 50 \text{ mm of mercury}$$

The easiest way to measure blood pressure is with a battery-operated monitor that fits over a person's index finger, wrist, or upper arm. It provides a digital display of both systolic and diastolic pressure. Still another battery-powered blood pressure monitor inflates at the press of a button and gives a digital display of blood pressure and pulse rate. Your family may have an instrument similar to one of those shown in Figure 3a or 3b. If not, you may be able to borrow one from a friend or from your science teacher or school nurse.

The more traditional device for measuring blood pressure is the sphygmomanometer (Figure 3c) found in doctors' offices. A sphygmo-manometer is more difficult to operate than the automatic devices. It consists of a cuff that is placed around the upper arm and then inflated. When the pressure in the cuff exceeds the pressure of the blood flowing through the brachial artery in the upper arm, the artery collapses and blood flow stops. By slowly reducing the pressure in the cuff, a point is reached at which systolic pressure forces a spurt of blood through the artery. The short spurt of blood produces a sound that can be heard by placing a stethoscope over the artery below the cuff on the inside of the elbow. When the first sound is heard, the pressure is read on a gauge attached to the cuff. As the pressure in the cuff continues to be slowly reduced, the sound becomes more muffled and eventually disappears when the cuff no longer restricts blood flow. Consequently, the pressure at which the sound disappears is the subject's diastolic blood pressure.

If possible, use one of the automatic blood pressure devices. Should you have to use a sphygmomanometer, **ask an adult** familiar with taking blood pressure to help you. **Be sure that the cuff does not restrict a subject's blood flow for more than a few seconds.**

Ask your volunteer to sit in a chair with one arm on a table. Determine the person's blood pressure with whichever instrument is available. What is the systolic blood pressure? What is the diastolic blood pressure? What is the pulse pressure?

Now, reverse roles. What is your blood pressure? What is your pulse pressure?

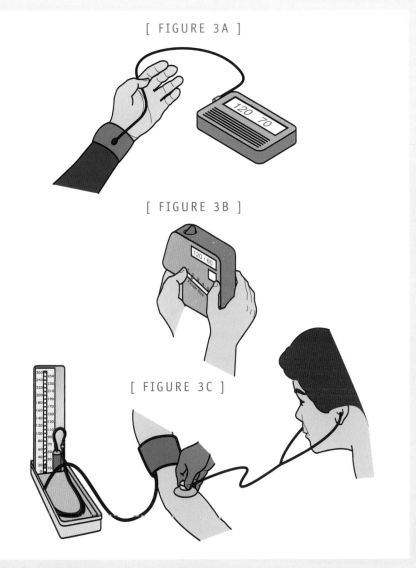

[FIGURE 3A]

[FIGURE 3B]

[FIGURE 3C]

These devices are used to measure blood pressure. a) An automatic cuff-type blood pressure and pulse monitor. A similar model fits over the upper arm. b) A finger-type automatic blood pressure and pulse monitor. c) A sphygmomanometer, such as those commonly found in a doctor's office.

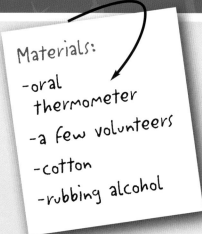

Materials:

- oral thermometer
- a few volunteers
- cotton
- rubbing alcohol

The temperature of a person's body can be determined with an oral thermometer such as one of those seen in Figure 4. **Use only nonmercury thermometers, such as those filled with alcohol. The liquid in some thermometers is mercury. It is dangerous to breathe mercury vapor.**

Use an oral thermometer to measure your body temperature. Most digital thermometers use a sound signal to indicate when the temperature has reached its maximum value and is no longer changing. What is your temperature?

After you use it, clean the thermometer with cotton soaked in rubbing alcohol. After the thermometer has dried, use it to measure someone else's body temperature. Is that person's temperature the same as yours? If not, does one of you have a fever?

Measure the body temperatures of a few healthy volunteers. Are they all the same? If not, by how many tenths of a degree do they differ? Do you agree with the statement, "Normal body temperature is 37°C, or 98.6°F"?

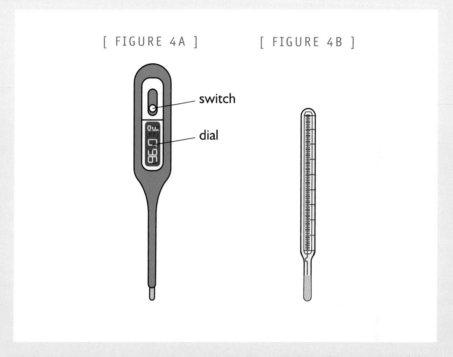

[FIGURE 4A]   [FIGURE 4B]

switch

dial

Body temperature may be measured with a digital thermometer (a) or a nonmercury thermometer (b).

Chapter 2

The Effects of Body Position, Exercise, and Conditioning

HOW DOES BODY POSITION AFFECT HEART RATE, BREATHING RATE, BODY TEMPERATURE, AND BLOOD PRESSURE? Does your heart beat faster when you stand up? Does exercise affect vital signs? Can physical conditioning change the way heart rate, breathing rate, body temperature, and blood pressure respond to changes in body position or to exercise? Does conditioning affect the amount of air you breathe? The experiments found in this chapter will help you answer these and other questions.

2.1 Body Position, Exercise, Conditioning, and Heart Rate

Materials:

- stopwatch, or clock or watch with second hand
- a partner
- notebook and pen or pencil
- a volunteer who is in very good physical condition
- a volunteer of the same weight, gender, and age who is not in very good physical condition
- graph paper

To save time, you can combine this experiment with the next two experiments (2.2 and 2.3). If you decide to do all three experiments together, you will need three partners, one to measure heart rate, a second to measure breathing rate, and a third to measure blood pressure. In this way, the data for three experiments can be obtained at the same time. If you have a blood pressure monitor that also records heart rate, you will need only two partners.

Lie on your back on a couch or floor and rest quietly for five minutes. Then have your partner take your pulse to determine your heart rate. Record that number in your notebook.

Sit up for five minutes. Again, have your partner take your pulse, then record the number in your notebook. Is your heart rate higher when you are sitting?

Now, stand for five minutes. Again, have your partner determine your heart rate and record the result. Does your heart beat faster when you are standing?

Run in place for five minutes. As soon as you stop running, stand still as your partner takes your pulse. After recording your heart rate, have your partner take your pulse and record your heart rate at one-minute intervals until it returns to the rate you had when standing before exercising.

Plot a graph of your heart rate in beats per minute versus time, in minutes, for the period following your exercise. One such graph is shown in Figure 5. How does it compare with the graph you made? What can you conclude from the graph you made?

Repeat this experiment with a volunteer who is in very good physical condition and with a volunteer of the same age, gender, and weight who is not. How do the data for the two volunteers compare?

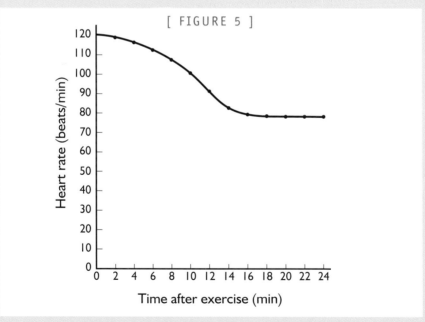

[FIGURE 5]

Time after exercise (min)

This graph shows a person's heart rate versus time, in minutes, after exercise. How does it compare with the graph you made?

2.2 How Do Conditioning and Exercise Affect Breathing Rate?

Materials:

- stopwatch, or clock or watch with second hand

- a partner

- notebook and pen or pencil

- a volunteer who is in very good physical condition

- a volunteer of the same age, gender, and weight who is not in very good physical condition

- graph paper

Lie on your back on a couch or floor and rest quietly for five minutes. After that time, your partner will watch your chest to determine how many times you breathe in one minute. Record that data in a notebook. What is your breathing rate while lying on your back?

Sit up and remain seated for five minutes. Again, have your partner determine your breathing rate after that time. Record the data. What is your breathing rate while sitting?

Stand up for five minutes and then have your partner determine your breathing rate. Record the data. What is your breathing rate when standing?

Next, run in place for five minutes. As soon as you stop running, stand still as your partner counts the number of breaths you take in fifteen seconds. How can that data be recorded as breaths per minute?

In the same way, have your partner determine your breathing rate at one-minute intervals until your breathing rate returns to the rate you had when standing before exercising. Record all the data.

Plot a graph of breathing rate in breaths per minute versus time, in minutes, for the period following your exercise. What can you conclude from the graph?

Repeat this experiment with a volunteer who is in very good physical condition and with a volunteer of the same age, gender, and weight who is not. How do the data for the two people compare?

Materials:
- a partner
- battery-powered automatic blood pressure device or sphygmomanometer and stethoscope
- notebook and pen or pencil
- clock or watch
- graph paper
- a volunteer who is in very good physical condition
- a volunteer of the same age, gender, and weight who is not in very good physical condition

Lie on your back on a couch or floor and rest quietly for five minutes. After that time, have your partner measure your blood pressure while you are still on your back. Record both your diastolic and systolic pressure. What is your blood pressure while lying on your back?

Next, sit up and remain seated for five minutes. While you are seated, have your partner measure your blood pressure. Record the data. What is your normal blood pressure while sitting?

Now, stand for five minutes. Have your partner measure your blood pressure as you stand. Record the data. What is your blood pressure while standing? What is your pulse pressure?

Next, run in place for five minutes. As soon as you stop running, stand still as your partner measures your blood pressure. Record that data in your notebook. What is your blood pressure immediately after exercising? What is your pulse pressure?

While you are standing, have your partner measure your blood pressure at three-minute intervals until your blood pressure is nearly the same as it was when standing before exercising. Record the data. Use that blood pressure data to plot a graph of systolic blood pressure versus time after exercising. Do the same for diastolic pressure. Use the same data to plot a graph of pulse pressure versus time after exercise. What can you conclude from these graphs?

Repeat this experiment with a volunteer who is in very good physical condition and with a volunteer of the same age, gender, and weight who is not. How do the data for the two people compare?

 Science Fair Project Idea

Measure the breathing rates, heart rates, and blood pressures of a number of different people after they have been lying, sitting, standing, and exercising for five minutes. Does a subject's age, weight, gender, or physical condition seem to affect the results? If so, how are the results related to these factors?

Materials:
- oral thermometer
- household thermometer
- vacuum cleaner
- clock or watch

Before you begin this experiment, do not exercise for at least an hour. Use an oral thermometer to measure your body temperature. Place the thermometer under your tongue for three minutes. What is your body temperature after you have been lying down for five minutes? What is your body temperature after sitting for five minutes? After standing for five minutes?

Now run in place for five minutes or until you are perspiring freely. Take your temperature again. Record your temperature at five-minute intervals. How long did it take before your temperature was the same as it was before exercising? Did your temperature change significantly after exercising? How much did it change? Can you explain why?

Now, compare your change in temperature with that of a machine, such as a vacuum cleaner. A vacuum cleaner pulls in air that passes through a filter (bag), over the motor, and out an opening at the back or top of the machine. To begin this part of the experiment, place a household thermometer at the opening where air emerges from the vacuum cleaner. What is the temperature at the opening? Continue to hold the thermometer in place as you turn on the vacuum cleaner. What happens to the temperature of the air coming out of the machine? Does the temperature become constant after the motor has run for some time? Why or why not?

How did the change in temperature of the air coming out of the vacuum cleaner compare with your temperature change following exercise? Can you explain any differences in these two temperature changes?

Science Fair Project Ideas

- Do some research at a library or on the Internet to find out how body temperature is controlled.
- Explain how a vacuum cleaner works. What must happen for it to pull in air?

2.5 How Is Body Temperature Maintained?

Materials:

- electric fan
- household thermometer
- small cotton cloth
- rubber bands
- tape
- plastic bag larger than your hand
- water
- place where you can exercise, such as gymnasium or yard

As you found in Experiment 2.4, your temperature does not change very much. Even when the heat of summer raises air temperatures above 100°F (38°C), your body temperature changes very little.

How can your temperature remain nearly constant even when the air around you is warmer than your body? Sitting in front of an electric fan helps to keep you cool, but does the fan cool the air?

To find out, hang a household thermometer near the center of the room to measure the temperature of the still air. After a few minutes, read and record the temperature. Next, turn on the fan. Watch the thermometer. Does the air get cooler?

If a fan does not cool the air, there must be some other reason moving air makes you feel cooler. Dip a small piece of cotton cloth into some lukewarm water. Then squeeze out the excess water. Wrap the cloth around the lower end of the thermometer. The cloth should completely cover the thermometer's bulb. Use a rubber band to hold the cloth in place. When the liquid in the thermometer stops moving, read and record the temperature. Then hang the thermometer in the wind generated by the fan. What happens to the temperature?

Leave the thermometer in front of the fan until the cloth is dry. What is the temperature when the cloth is thoroughly dry? How does it compare with the temperature of the air in the room when the fan is turned off?

What causes the temperature of the wet cloth to decrease? To find out, spread a few drops of water on the back of one of your hands. Leave the other hand dry. Hold both hands in the moving air coming from a fan. Which hand feels cooler?

Repeat the experiment when both hands are dry. Do both hands feel about the same now?

You may have seen a wet road or sidewalk become dry after a rainstorm. The water evaporates; it changes from a liquid to a gas. You may also have noticed that the water evaporates faster when a wind is blowing. The same thing happened to the water on your hand when you held it near the fan.

Water, like all substances, is made up of molecules. These tiny particles of matter move faster when they are heated. The higher the temperature, the faster they move. The water molecules on your hand absorbed heat from your body. As they did, the faster moving ones escaped into the air and were carried away by the wind from the fan, leaving the slower (cooler) ones behind to absorb more heat from your body.

Normally, when you are hot, you perspire. The sweat absorbs heat from your body as it evaporates. This helps keep your body cool. If the wind is blowing, sweat evaporates faster from your body and you feel even cooler. What happens when the air is very humid, that is, when there is a lot of moisture in the air? To find out you can do some other experiments.

A HAND IN A BAG

Put one of your hands inside a plastic bag. Use tape to seal the mouth of the bag around your wrist. Then go for a run. As you begin to sweat, which hand feels warmer? What do you see collecting on the inside surface of the plastic bag? How can you explain your observation?

Later, when you are cool and at rest, cover your hand with another plastic bag. Seal it as before and continue to wear it for an hour or so while you read or sit quietly. At the end of this period, carefully examine the bag on your hand. What evidence do you have that water evaporates from your body even when you are at rest?

2.6 Perspiration and Weight

Materials:

- water
- drinking glass
- light, loose clothing
- bathroom scale
- towel
- place where you can exercise, such as gymnasium or yard

You have seen that water in the form of perspiration appears on your skin when you exercise. Exercise requires energy, and much of the energy is released as heat, which tends to raise your body temperature. Your body responds by forming beads of perspiration that evaporate and cool your body. But how much weight do you lose by sweating?

For this experiment, use the bathroom before you begin and try not to use it again until you have finished the experiment. Fully hydrate yourself by drinking about ½ liter (one pint or two large glasses) of water two hours before exercising and another glass of water half an hour before exercising. Remove your clothes and weigh yourself. Record your exact weight in your notebook. Put on light, loose clothing.

Exercise vigorously for at least half an hour. You might run, play a competitive game of basketball, do calisthenics, or engage in any other form of exercise that will make you perspire. After exercising, remove your clothes and dry yourself thoroughly with a towel before weighing yourself again. Record your weight. How much weight did you lose? What percentage of your body weight did you lose?

If possible, repeat this experiment under different weather conditions. How does your weight loss on a cool, dry day compare with your weight loss on a hot, humid day? How about on a dry, hot day?

Materials:

- a partner
- 2 large, rigid, transparent or semitransparent plastic containers, one with a volume of about 4 liters (1 gallon) and another about twice as large
- a glass or plastic plate large enough to cover the mouths of both containers
- dish pan
- kitchen sink
- tape
- marking pen
- large graduated cylinder or measuring cup
- 1-liter or 1-quart plastic bag
- rubber tubing about 30 cm (12 in) long
- a short length of glass or rigid plastic tubing
- cotton gauze or cotton balls
- rubbing alcohol
- twist tie
- calculator (optional)
- notebook and pen or pencil
- several volunteers of different ages, genders, heights, weights, and chest sizes

The oxygen that the muscles of our bodies need in order to function is obtained from the air we breathe into our lungs. The more air we can breathe, the greater the amount of oxygen that can reach our blood and be carried to muscles and other tissues.

The volume of air we breathe can be measured with a device known as a spirometer (see Figure 6). You probably don't have access to a spirometer, but you can make reasonably accurate measurements with a plastic bag and a pail of water or with a one-gallon, water-filled container and a piece of rubber tubing.

The volume of air you normally inhale and exhale is called your *tidal air*. The extra air you can inhale if you take a deep breath following a normal breath is called your *complemental air*. The volume of air you can force from your lungs after exhaling normally is called your *supplemental air*. After you have forced the supplemental air from your lungs, about 1 liter (1.1 quarts) of *residual air* remains in your lungs.

To measure your tidal air, calibrate a large (4-liter or 1-gallon) rigid, transparent or semitransparent plastic container. To calibrate it, first place a strip of narrow tape vertically along the side of the container. Then pour known volumes of water into the container and mark the water levels of the different volumes with a marking pen.

Pour some water into the container until the level is on one of the lines you marked. Hold your nose so that all the air you breathe goes through your mouth. When you have adjusted to mouth breathing, place the opening of a 1-liter or 1-quart plastic bag (from which all the air has been removed) firmly around your mouth just before you exhale.

Collect the exhaled air in the bag. (Do not blow. Just exhale in a normal way.) Twist the neck of the bag to seal off the exhaled air, and secure it with a twist tie. **Caution: Never pull a plastic bag over your head.**

Hold the bag of air in your hand and push it under the water in the calibrated container as shown in Figure 7. Have a partner use a felt pen to mark the water level in the container before and after submerging the bag. Also mark your wrist at the water level. Finally, squeeze all the air out of

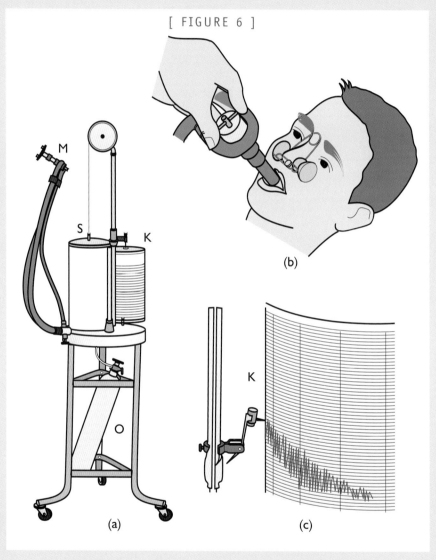

[FIGURE 6]

(b)

(a)

(c)

a) A drawing of a spirometer. M is the mouthpiece; S is the spirometer bell; K is the kymograph where the volume of air inhaled and exhaled is recorded; O is the oxygen tank, which can be used to measure the volume of oxygen used by a subject. b) The part of the spirometer that fits into a person's mouth. c) A view of a record being made on the kymograph.

the bag, hold the bag in your fist, put your fist back into the water up to the mark on your wrist, and have your partner mark the water level again. What is the volume of your hand and the empty bag? What is the volume of your tidal air?

SUPPLEMENTAL AIR

To measure the volume of your supplemental air, completely fill the 4-liter (1-gallon) container with water. Cover the mouth of the container with a glass or plastic plate. Next turn the container upside down and place its neck under the water in a dish pan that rests in a kitchen sink (see Figure 8).

Insert a short length of glass or rigid plastic tubing into a 30-cm (12-in) length of rubber tubing. Use a piece of cotton gauze to wipe the end of the glass or plastic tube with rubbing alcohol. This tube will serve

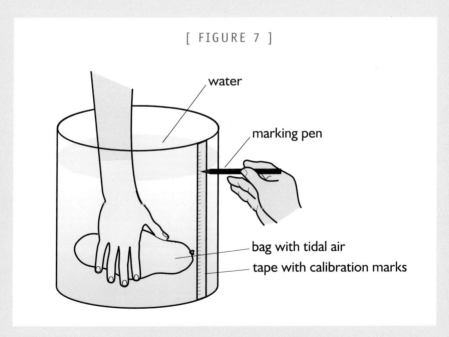

[FIGURE 7]

water

marking pen

bag with tidal air

tape with calibration marks

Measuring the volume of tidal air

as a mouth piece. Once the alcohol has evaporated, have a partner support the water-filled container while you place the end of the rubber
tubing up through the submerged mouth of the container. Hold the
mouth piece with your thumb and fingers as you breathe normally. After
exhaling normally, force as much air as possible from your lungs through
the mouth piece and rubber tubing and into the container. The supplemental air from your lungs will replace water from the container into the
dish pan. When you have forcibly exhaled as much air as possible, pinch
the rubber tubing with your fingers and remove it from the container.

Have your partner cover the submerged mouth of the partially filled
container, remove it from the pan, and turn it upright. You can then use
a graduated cylinder or measuring cup to measure the volume of water
needed to fill the container. This is, of course, equal to the volume of
air—your supplemental air—that you blew into the container. What is
the volume of your supplemental air?

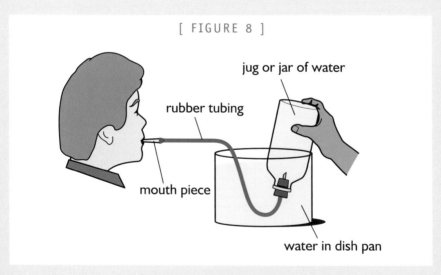

[FIGURE 8]

jug or jar of water

rubber tubing

mouth piece

water in dish pan

Measuring supplemental air

VITAL CAPACITY

A person's *vital capacity* is the volume of air that he or she can forcibly exhale after taking the deepest inhalation possible. You can determine your vital capacity with the same equipment you used to measure your supplemental air.

Again, clean the mouth piece with gauze moistened with alcohol while your partner fills the 8-liter (2-gallon) container with water and places it in the dish pan. Place the end of the rubber tube through the submerged mouth of the container. Now, inhale as much air as you possibly can. Then exhale as much air as you can through the mouth piece and into the container. Once you have exhaled as much air as possible, pinch the rubber tubing and remove it from the container. Your partner will cover the submerged mouth of the partially filled container, remove it from the pan, and turn it upright. You can then use a graduated cylinder or measuring cup to measure the volume of water needed to fill the container. What is your vital capacity?

Repeat the experiment to find your partner's vital capacity.

From all your measurements, what is the maximum volume of air that your lungs can hold? (Don't forget the 1 liter of residual air.) What is the maximum volume of air that your partner's lungs can hold?

Compare the vital capacities of a number of volunteers. Are these volumes related to age? To gender? To height or weight? To chest size?

Compare the vital capacities of a number of volunteers who are in good physical condition with the vital capacities of people of comparable size, age, and gender who are not in good physical condition. Is vital capacity related to a person's physical condition?

Science Fair Project Ideas

- Show that a person's vital capacity is the sum of his or her complemental, tidal, and supplemental airs.
- How can you calculate the volume of air you breathe in one day?
- How do scientists determine the volume of residual air? Is it related to a person's size?
- Design and conduct experiments to determine the effect of smoking on vital capacity. Does smoking have any effect on tidal air? On supplemental air? On complemental air?

Chapter 3

Metabolism and Nutrition

IN THE PAST THIRTY YEARS, OBESITY IN THE UNITED STATES HAS INCREASED DRASTICALLY. Today, approximately 66 percent of adults are overweight or obese and 17 percent of children and adolescents (ages 2–19 years) are overweight. Being overweight can lead to heart disease, diabetes, and many other physical problems. Consequently, it makes good sense to exercise and eat a healthy diet. It is also important to limit the size of your portions and the amount of snack foods and sugary drinks you consume.

A calorie is the unit scientists use to measure the energy content of foods. One calorie is defined as the quantity of energy that is required to raise the temperature of 1 gram of water 1°C. Be careful not to confuse this calorie with the one you see written on the labels of food products. The calorie content of foods as reported on the label is not the same as the calorie used by scientists. To avoid confusion, the scientific version should be written with a lowercase *c* (calorie), whereas the dietetic version should be written with an uppercase *C* (Calorie). One Calorie actually equals 1,000 calories. This distinction, however, is not always clear. The next time you have a can of soda in your hands, check the label. If it is not a diet soda, it may say that one serving contains 100 *calories*. But that is actually 100 *Calories* or 100,000 *calories*.

Participating in sports is one good way to burn calories and have fun at the same time. However, excess weight requires the heart to pump harder and faster to supply all the extra flesh with blood. Consequently, exercise should be accompanied by proper nutrition. A healthy diet includes fruits, vegetables, grains, lowfat dairy products, fish, and lean meat. Junk food, which is often rich in fats, sugar, and salt, should be avoided.

In this chapter, you will find basic information about how we use food in our bodies. You will also learn how to perform simple tests to find out if you are overweight. You will learn about the calories that common daily activities require. You will design a healthy diet and learn how to read nutritional facts on food labels and know what they mean.

3.1　What Is Your Basal Metabolic Rate?

Metabolism is the body's use of food after it has been digested and transported to cells. Our body cells use food as a source of energy and as raw materials for building the complex molecules we need to live.

Metabolic rate is the speed at which our bodies release the energy stored in food. It is usually expressed as Calories per hour (Cal/h) or Calories per day (Cal/day).

A person's basal metabolic rate (BMR) is the rate at which energy must be produced just to keep the body alive. It is measured when the subject is awake, lying down, and at rest in a warm room, 12 to 18 hours after eating any food. The rate can be measured directly by placing the subject in a chamber where the heat is calculated by the change in temperature of water that is circulated through the chamber. Heat released by the body warms the water. By knowing the amount of water and its temperature change, the heat released by the body can be calculated.

BMR can also be determined indirectly by measuring the volume of oxygen (O_2) consumed and carbon dioxide (CO_2) produced per hour by a subject. Scientists have found the volume of CO_2 divided by the volume of O_2 can be used to determine the energy released.

From direct measurements, we know that a person's BMR depends on surface area; that is, the area of the skin that covers the body. The larger a person's surface area, the more heat that is lost to the cooler air surrounding the body. To keep the body temperature constant, heat must be produced to replace that which is lost. BMR also depends on gender. It is greater for males than females. And, as we grow older, our BMR decreases. BMR depends, too, on the amount of thyroid hormone the body produces and on body temperature. A fever of 1°C (1.8°F) increases the BMR by about 13 percent. People who secrete more than normal amounts of thyroid hormone have higher metabolic rates. Those who secrete less than normal amounts of thyroid hormone have lower metabolic rates. Finally, emotions and drugs, such as caffeine, can increase an individual's metabolic rate.

Generally, a person's BMR can be closely approximated from age, gender, and surface area. Table 1 shows how basal metabolism per square meter (m^2) of body area is related to gender and age. The graph in Figure 9 provides a way to find a body's surface area from height and weight. By using the table and the graph, you can find the expected BMR for any individual.

Suppose a 13-year-old boy weighs 110 pounds and is 5 feet 3 inches tall. What can we expect his BMR to be? From Table 1, we see that a 13-year-old boy, on the average, burns 50 Calories every hour for each square meter of body area. To find the boy's body area, we look at Figure 9.

TABLE 1.

Age (years)	Calories per hour for each square meter of body area ($Cal/h/m^2$)	
	Male	Female
2–12	52	50
13–14	50	46
15–16	46	43
17–18	43	40
19–20	41	38
21–40	40	37
41–60	38	36

*Adapted from Table 26-5 of *Anthony's Textbook of Anatomy & Physiology*, Thibodeau, Gary A., and Kevin T. Patton, St. Louis, Miss.: Mosby-Year Book, 1994.

The graph uses meters to measure height and kilograms for weight. So we must first change inches (in) to meters (m) and pounds (lb) to kilograms (kg). Since 39.37 in = 1.0 m and 2.2 lb = 1.0 kg,

63 in ÷ 39.37 in/m = 1.6 m and 110 lb ÷ 2.2 lb/kg = 50 kg

The graph shows us that a person who weighs 50 kg and is 1.6 m tall has a surface area of almost 1.5 square meters (m^2). His BMR, therefore, is approximately

1.5 m^2 x 50 Cal/h/m^2 = 75 Cal/h or 1,800 Cal/day

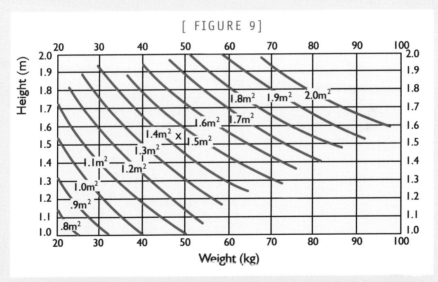

[FIGURE 9]

To determine the surface area of the body, find a person's weight on the horizontal axis. Then go up that vertical weight line to the horizontal line that represents the person's height. The intersection of those two lines, on or near the curved lines showing area, is surface area. For example, say a person weighs 48 kg and is 1.55 m tall. The weight and height lines meet at a point shown as an "X" on the graph. Since this point is about midway between the curves representing 1.4 m^2 and 1.5 m^2, we estimate the surface area to be 1.45 m^2.

The value calculated in this example is an average for the person described. However, other factors, such as the amount of thyroid hormone secreted, body temperature, caffeine, and emotions can affect an individual's BMR.

Use Table 1 and Figure 9 to calculate your BMR. What is the BMR of each of your volunteers? Do you suspect that any of these people have a BMR that is actually higher than the one you calculated? If so, what makes you think so? Do you suspect that any of them have a BMR that is lower than the one you calculated?

3.2 What Is Your Total Metabolic Rate?

Materials:

-a few volunteers

-notebook and pen or pencil

-Tables 2 and 3

-calculator (optional)

Total metabolic rate is the energy required by the body per unit of time. It is usually expressed as Calories per hour or Calories per day. It includes the BMR, which is often more than half of the total metabolic rate, as well as the energy needed for muscles to carry out all the activities we do each day. It involves, too, the effect of food on metabolism.

After we eat, our metabolic rate increases because energy is required to metabolize the food. Table 2 provides information that can be used to estimate the total metabolic rate and the energy needed for an entire day's activity.

Consider an active 50-kg boy who sleeps for 10 hours, studies for 3 hours, sits in classes for 4 hours, watches television for 1 hour, spends an hour walking to and from school, plays baseball for 2 hours, rides his bike for an hour to travel 10 miles, does yard work for 1 hour, and reads in a chair for an hour. A summary of the boy's activities and energy requirements is listed in Table 2.

TABLE 2.

Activities and Energy Requirements of 50-kg Boy

Activity	Energy required (Hours x energy in Cal/kg per hour x body weight = Cal)
Sleeping	10 x 0.80 x 50 = 400
Studying	3 x 2.5 x 50 = 375
Sitting in class	4 x 1.3 x 50 = 260
Sitting for TV	1 x 0.9 x 50 = 45
Walking	1 x 4.4 x 50 = 220
Playing baseball	2 x 4.6 x 50 = 460
Biking	1 x 7 x 50 = 350
Doing yard work	1 x 3.1 x 50 = 155
Reading	1 x 2.0 x 50 = 100
Total:	24 hr; 2,365 Cal

TABLE 3. Energy Required to Perform Various Activities

Activity	Average energy per kilogram of weight (Cal/kg) to carry on the activity for 1 hour
Baseball	4.6
Basketball	6.2
Bicycling (10 miles per hour)	7.0
Dancing	4.4
Eating	1.3
Football	7.5
Golf	4.8
Housework	3.5
Jogging	5.5
Judo, wrestling, karate	11.0
Office work	2.6
Reading	2.0
Reclining	0.9
Running	11.0
Skating	9.0
Skiing	8.4
Soccer	7.8
Sleeping	0.8
Swimming	6.3
Sitting at rest	2.0
Sitting in class	1.3
Studying	2.5
Standing	1.3
Tennis	8.2
Walking	4.4
Watching television	0.9
Yard work	3.1

Keep a record of your own activities for an average day. Then use Table 3 to estimate your energy requirements for that day. How do they compare with those given in Table 4? Were you more or less active than the average person your age?

Ask a few volunteers to keep records of their daily activities. Then show them how to calculate their energy requirements.

TABLE 4.

Average Daily Energy Requirements for People of Different Ages and Genders

Person	Energy needed for one day (Cal)
Infant: 2–9 months	1,000
Child: 8 years old	2,100
Boy: 15 years old	3,000
Girl: 15 years old	2,500
Woman: inactive	1,900
Woman: active	2,200
Man: inactive	2,500
Man: active	3,000

3.3 What Diet Meets Your Energy Requirements?

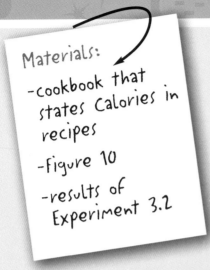

Materials:
- cookbook that states Calories in recipes
- Figure 10
- results of Experiment 3.2

The energy you need to carry out your activities, such as those you recorded in Experiment 3.2, comes from the food you eat. For example, a slice of white bread provides 70 Calories of energy when it is metabolized in your body. The energy available from servings of various foods can be found in many cookbooks. But foods provide more than energy. They also contain vitamins and minerals that are essential for good health and chemicals that are used to build new tissue and complex substances needed for life.

A food pyramid, such as the one shown in Figure 10, clarifies the kinds and amounts of food you need to maintain good health. It is also important to remember that fats and sugars should be used sparingly. Eat plenty of grains, such as whole-grain cereal, breads, and pasta. Fill your plate with a variety of brightly colored vegetables. When you reach for a snack, choose a piece of fruit. Make sure you get enough calcium by drinking milk and eating yogurt and cheese, beans, nuts and seeds (such as almonds and sesame), leafy green vegetables, oranges, figs, salmon, and sardines (see Experiment 3.5). Don't forget protein; Make sure you eat at least 5 ounces of meat, chicken, turkey, fish, or beans daily.

Do some research on food values and, considering your own energy use, use the cookbook to design a diet that meets all your nutritional needs.

[FIGURE 10]

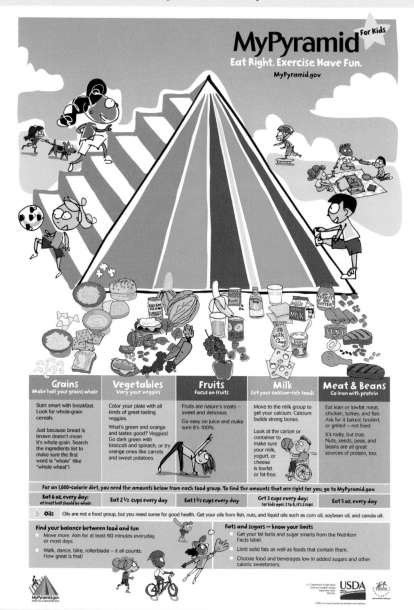

MyPyramid provides recommended types and amounts of different foods. It also reminds kids to be physically active every day and to make healthy food choices.

CARBOHYDRATE LOADING

Carbohydrates are found in such foods as pasta, fruits, vegetables, and grains. The digestion of complex carbohydrates, such as the starch in pasta, begins in the mouth and continues in the stomach and small intestine. The end product of this digestive process is glucose, a soluble sugar that is absorbed by the blood and carried to the cells of the body. Some glucose is converted to glycogen, an insoluble starch that is stored in muscles and the liver. Excess glucose is stored as fat.

During exercise, glucose is "burned" in the body to provide energy. As the concentration of glucose in the blood decreases, the pancreas secretes glucagon. Glucagon causes cells in the liver to convert glycogen to glucose, which tends to raise the amount of glucose in the blood and provide the "fuel" needed for muscular action.

Some athletes who participate in endurance sports (events that take two or more hours of steady exercise), such as distance running, eat large amounts of carbohydrates prior to competition, a practice known as *carbohydrate loading*. Some simply eat a dinner of pasta, potatoes, rice, and bread, along with fruits and vegetables, the night before the athletic event. Others believe it is best to remove most of the body's glycogen before loading the body with carbohydrates. These athletes exercise vigorously about six days before the competition to reduce their body's glycogen supply. They then eat a high-protein, low-carbohydrate diet for three days to keep their glycogen level low. The theory is that starving the liver and muscle cells of glycogen for several days stimulates them to store excess amounts of glycogen. For three days before the event, these athletes provide their bodies with extra glycogen by eating foods rich in carbohydrates.

ASSESSING NUTRITIONAL VALUE OF FOODS

A container or package of food is required by law to carry a set of nutritional facts that provides valuable information. The facts may include serving size; Calories; the quantities of various nutrients such as sugar, protein, fat, vitamins, and minerals; the percentage of the daily amounts required for a balanced diet; and other information related to the specific food. Some foods, such as meats, vegetables, and fruits, do not bear nutritional labels, but it is easy to find their nutrient content either in a book or on the Internet. Using the information available from food labels and other sources may help you improve your diet and, consequently, your overall health.

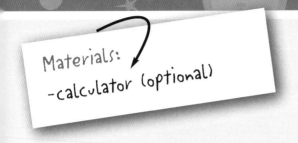

Materials:
-calculator (optional)

Food labels are designed to help you choose foods that provide the nutrients you need for good health. They are based upon the Dietary Guidelines for Americans developed by the United States Department of Agriculture (USDA). A lot of information is provided regarding sugar, salt, fat, cholesterol, dietary fiber, carbohydrate, protein, and vitamin and mineral content. *Daily value (DV)* is a reference value that serves as a guideline for comparing products.

A reprint of the "Nutritional Facts" from the back of a can of sardines in mustard sauce is presented in Figure 11. To see how you can make use of this information, consider first the weight of the sardines. A label on the can gives the net weight in ounces (oz) as well as in grams (g). There are 28.4 g in one ounce. What net weight, in ounces, will also be listed on the can?

The percent daily value shows how much of a nutrient one serving of the product provides in a day's average, healthy consumption for an adult who needs to eat 2,000 Calories each day to maintain weight and stay healthy. The percent daily value is not a recommendation for anyone. Maybe you are growing and need more Calories. Maybe you are older and need fewer. Age and gender affect the body's needs for minerals; young women need more iron than older women do, for example, and teenage girls need more iron than boys do. The percent daily value is a general guideline to use in comparing products. How? The sardine label shows that one serving provides 35 percent, on average, of the saturated fat that a person eating 2,000 Calories a day can safely consume. That means that—after eating the sardines—it makes sense to choose foods lower in saturated fat for the rest of the day. On the other hand, the sardines contain 0 percent of the daily value of vitamins A and C. That

[FIGURE 11]

Sardines in Mustard Sauce	
Nutritional Facts	
Serving size 1 can (120 g)	
Calories 210	**Calories from fat 120**
	Percent of Daily Value*
Total Fat 13 g	20%
Saturated Fat 7 g	35%
Cholesterol 95 g	32%
Sodium 460 mg	19%
Total Carbohydrate 2 g	1%
Dietary Fiber 0 g	0%
Sugars 0 g	0%
Protein 22 g	44%
Vitamin A	0%
Calcium	40%
Iron	40%
Vitamin C	0%
*Percent daily values (DV) are based on a 2,000-calorie diet.	

Nutritional facts found on a food label provide useful information about sardines in mustard sauce.

suggests that eating fruits and vegetables rich in those vitamins would be wise.

Daily values are not shown on the label, but you can find them in tables put out by the USDA. For example, the daily value for calcium is 1,000 mg. Using that information and the percentage on the label, can you calculate how much calcium, in grams, is in the sardines?

Study the sardine can label. How many grams are in one can of sardines? How many Calories does the can of sardines provide? How many of those Calories are from fat? You can answer these questions by reading directly off the label.

Notice that the label says that 120 of the Calories in one serving of sardines come from fat. Notice, also, that each serving contains 13 grams of fat. Given those two facts, the number of Calories in 1 gram of fat can be calculated.

$$120 \div 13 = 9.2$$

How could you determine the number of Calories from saturated fat in one serving of the sardines?

How can you determine the daily value of a nutrient when it is not given on the label? Try this example: One serving of sardines provides 22 grams of protein, which is 44 percent of the daily value. Therefore, 0.44 times the daily value is 22 grams. The daily value can be found as 22/0.44 = 50 grams.

Find the daily value of sodium and cholesterol using a similar strategy.

According to the data given, how much energy, in Calories, can be obtained from 1 gram of fat? In the sardines, what percentage of the fat is saturated fat?

If a person already gets 2.4 grams of sodium per day from other foods, should he or she include a serving of sardines as a source of sodium with every lunch? Why or why not?

The daily Caloric intake for a teenager varies depending on a number of things, including physical activity. If we assume it is about 2,000

Calories, what percent of a teenager's daily Caloric intake can be obtained from a can of sardines in mustard sauce?

The label on a 16-oz (453-g) jar of all-natural peanut butter (no added salt, sugar, or oils) is given in Figure 12. Based on the data on the peanut butter label:

- How many Calories are in one tablespoonful of the peanut butter?
- If you put 3 tablespoonfuls of peanut butter on a piece of bread, what fraction of your daily value of total fat has been spread on the bread? How many Calories are in the peanut butter?
- You would get almost one fifth of your day's sodium from a single serving of sardines. Would peanut butter be a good food choice for that day if you were trying to follow sodium intake guidelines?
- If you eat 240 grams of sardines and 4 tablespoons of peanut butter in a day, what percent of the daily value of fat have you consumed? Should you eat other foods that are high in fat?
- How much of the carbohydrate in peanut butter is not sugar?

Science Fair Project Idea

Examine the labels on a variety of cookies at a food store. In terms of nutritional value, which cookies would be the best ones to eat? Which ones would be the least nutritious? Explain your choices.

[FIGURE 12]

Natural Peanut Butter	
Nutritional Facts	
Serving size 2 Tbsp (32 g)	
Servings Per Container 14	
Amount Per Serving	
Calories 190	Calories from fat 150
	Percent of Daily Value*
Total Fat 16 g	24%
Saturated Fat 2 g	11%
Trans Fat 0 g	
Polyunsaturated Fat 5 g	
Monounsaturated Fat 8 g	
Cholesterol 0 mg	0%
Sodium 0 mg	0%
Total Carbohydrate 7 g	2%
Dietary Fiber 3 g	8%
Sugars 2 g	
Protein 9 g	
Vitamin A	0%
Vitamin C	0%
Calcium	2%
Iron	4%
*Percent daily values (DV) are based on a 2,000-calorie diet.	

The nutritional facts on a peanut butter label provide information about Calories, fat, carbohydrates, protein, vitamins, and more.

Materials:
- notebook and pen or pencil
- calculator (optional)
- Table 5
- some of the foods listed in Table 5

You need larger amounts of calcium than any other mineral. Calcium is a major component in the minerals that make up two thirds of the weight of your bones. Without calcium you cannot build the strong bones that provide the support your body needs. Nor can you grow the teeth that allow you to bite and chew food. Doctors advise pre-teenagers and teenagers to consume 1,200 to 1,500 mg (1.2 to 1.5 g) of calcium each day.

As Table 5 reveals, dairy foods are one of the richest sources of calcium. Other good sources include dark green leafy vegetables such as kale, beet and turnip greens, broccoli, chard, and acorn squash. Unfortunately, some foods prevent calcium from being absorbed from the intestines. Chocolate, almonds, Swiss chard, and rhubarb contain oxalic acid, which combines with calcium to form calcium oxalate, a chemical the kidneys excrete.

Some people cannot drink milk because they are unable to digest lactose, or milk sugar. They are said to be *lactose intolerant*. They can, however, eat or drink lactose-free foods such as Lactaid milk, which contains as much calcium as real milk. Other foods, such as cereal, orange juice, soybeans, and bread are often fortified with calcium. Those who follow a *vegan* diet (a vegetarian diet that excludes animal products such as eggs, milk, and cheese) should monitor their calcium intake regularly. Calcium supplements should be taken in several small doses because the body cannot utilize more than 500 mg at a time. Furthermore, acid is needed to

TABLE 5.

Foods That Contain Calcium, Their Calcium Content, and the Calories per Serving

Food source	Calcium (mg)	Calories
Dairy		
8 ounces (1 cup) of skim milk	350	85
8 ounces (1 cup) of whole milk	350	160
1 cup of lowfat fruit yogurt	372	250
1 ounce of light cream cheese	32	70
1 ounce of cheddar cheese	200	110
1 cup of vanilla ice cream	170	360
0.5 cup of lowfat cottage cheese	70	80
Nondairy		
1 cup of cooked broccoli	90	50
1 cup of soybeans	180	300
1 cup of fortified orange juice	300	110
1 cup of turnip or beet greens	180	30
1 cup of white beans	130	250
1 cup of tempeh (soybean cakes)	150	330
3 ounces of sardines (bones in)	350	190
3 ounces of canned salmon (bones in)	200	130

release the calcium so that it can be absorbed. Since stomach acid is secreted in response to food, supplements are best taken with meals.

Advertisements may tell you that you can take antacids as a calcium supplement because they contain calcium (in the form of calcium carbonate), which is true. The calcium carbonate, however, neutralizes some of the stomach acid. Many nutritionists recommend a supplement that contains calcium citrate because it has no effect on stomach acid and is readily absorbed.

Vitamin D is needed to maintain the proper concentration of calcium in the body. Consequently, an adequate supply of vitamin D is essential if your bones and teeth are to receive a sufficient amount of calcium. If you spend a reasonable amount of time outdoors, you probably have sufficient vitamin D, because vitamin D is made by your body when sunlight falls on your skin. At least fifteen minutes of sun exposure in the summer for a light skinned person is needed to make enough vitamin D. Longer periods of sun exposure are needed during the other seasons, and for people with darker skin.

Use the information provided in Table 5 to determine how many servings of each of the following foods you need to meet your daily calcium requirement: (1) skim milk, (2) whole milk, (3) vanilla ice cream, (4) low-fat cottage cheese, (5) broccoli, (6) fortified orange juice, (7) soybeans, (8) beet greens, and (9) sardines.

In meeting your daily calcium requirements, how many Calories would you also obtain from each of these foods?

Examine the labels on some of the packaged foods listed in Table 5. For each of the foods, what fraction of your daily requirements for other nutrients would you obtain from one serving of each food?

Science Fair Project Ideas

- Is it possible to get too much calcium? That is, can a large excess of calcium be harmful?
- Devise some nutrition tips for increasing the amount of calcium in a teenager's diet.

Chapter 4

Eating Habits to Maintain a Healthy Weight

CARBOHYDRATES MAKE UP THE BULK OF THE FOOD WE CONSUME AND PROVIDE MOST OF THE ENERGY OUR BODIES NEED. However, you cannot live for long on a diet of only carbohydrates. You need protein for growth and repair of cells. Enzymes are an important type of protein in your body. Enzymes help digest food and regulate vital chemical processes. Fat also has important functions in the body. It makes up cell membranes. The fatty tissue beneath the skin helps to insulate the body. Fat covering internal organs, such as the kidneys and stomach, serves as a protective cushion. It acts much like the pads worn by players in contact sports. Excess fat is stored in adipose tissue. Cells that contain a lot of fat have a soft texture. Such tissue is found just beneath the skin, in bone marrow and organs, and between muscle cells.

Most of our body fat is white fat, similar to the fat you find in meat. Tiny amounts of brown fat, which is darker and serves as a source of heat, are found in the middle of your chest and back.

Some fat accumulates in arteries. If it clogs or blocks arteries in the heart and brain, it can obstruct blood flow and cause a heart attack or stroke. Fat stored in adipose tissue is a reserve of energy that is used when food intake is not sufficient to meet energy needs. Fat is an efficient way to store energy because it provides more than twice the energy per gram of carbohydrates or proteins.

Food provides the energy and matter we need to keep our bodies warm, do work, and grow new cells. Even while we sleep, the energy produced by burning food is equivalent to the energy produced by a 75-watt lightbulb. If the energy present in the food a person eats equals the energy needed to maintain the body, a person's weight does not change. If the energy present in the food a person eats is less than the energy needed to maintain the body, that person will lose weight. The extra energy the body needs comes from stored fat. If the energy present in the food a person eats exceeds the energy needed to maintain the body, that person will gain weight. The extra food energy is stored in body cells as fat.

Aside from hormonal disorders and disease, obesity is the long-term result of eating too much food or engaging in too little exercise. What one eats is as important as the quantity of food eaten. To avoid excessive weight gain, which can lead to obesity, a person should eat no more food than is needed to meet his or her energy and growth needs. A person who wants to lose excess weight must reduce food intake, exercise more to increase the need for energy, or do both.

ENERGY STORAGE AND USE IN THE BODY

After a meal, carbohydrates are digested and a large amount of glucose sugar (a monosaccharide) enters the bloodstream and travels directly to the liver. Some goes on to fuel body cells immediately. Some is removed, converted to glycogen (a polysaccharide), and stored for later use. Excess glucose is converted to fat and sent into long-term storage.

As the concentration of glucose in the blood rises, the pancreas responds by secreting the hormone *insulin*. Increased insulin in the blood causes most body cells to absorb glucose. As glucose is burned by body cells to provide energy, the concentration of glucose in the blood decreases. As the concentration of glucose in the blood drops below normal, the pancreas secretes another hormone called *glucagon*. Glucagon stimulates cells in the liver to convert glycogen to glucose, which tends to raise the amount of glucose in the blood. Glucagon can also cause adipose tissue to break its fat into fatty acids and glycerin, which travel to the liver where the chemicals are converted to glucose. The antagonistic effects of glucagon and insulin maintain glucose at a set level.

Nervous signals indicating hunger and satiety (fullness) originate in the *hypothalamus*, a small organ at the base of the brain. If the center for hunger in an animal's hypothalamus is destroyed, the animal will starve; if the center for satiety is destroyed, the animal will eat itself to obesity. The hypothalamus also controls the rate of heat loss from the body. In a cold environment, it sends signals to blood vessels that divert the blood from the skin to the body's interior, thus reducing heat loss. If body temperature rises, the blood is sent to the skin to increase heat loss. Signals from the hypothalamus that lead to the pituitary and from there to the thyroid gland regulate the rate at which food is oxidized to release the heat that keeps the body warm.

Some people who are overweight produce too much insulin. As a result, the concentration of glucose in the blood is low and the hypothalamus sends hunger signals to the brain. For early humans, extra insulin was an advantage because it led them to eat in excess on those rare occasions when food was available in large quantities. Those people were so physically active seeking food and shelter that obesity was not a problem. The problem was avoiding predators while finding enough food to survive.

Obese people may have muscle cells that resist glucose absorption and adipose tissue that is receptive to the same sugar, which is converted to fat and stored. For such people, exercise is essential even though added weight makes exercise more difficult. Exercise adds muscle cells that take more of the glucose and leave less of it available for fat cells. Of course, the added exercise must be accompanied by a low-Calorie diet; otherwise, exercise may simply increase appetite and food consumption.

Some social and psychological factors foster obesity. Eating makes a person feel better; consequently, eating is a way to avoid dealing with other problems such as schoolwork, difficulty making friends, family strife, depression, and so on. Furthermore, social events are often followed by, or centered on, food. People who eat at a restaurant may feel they have to get their money's worth, and so they eat more food than they need. In addition, many people snack while they read or watch television, or they eat to be polite or to please whoever prepared the food.

Saying no to food is often difficult, but being overweight has many disadvantages. Fat people find that society, however wrong it may be, is predisposed to treat them unfairly. Obesity sometimes makes participation in sports difficult or even dangerous. Added weight leads to high blood pressure, heart disease, strokes, gallstones, diabetes, damage to joints that have to support the extra weight and difficulty coping with hot weather. It presents problems for surgeons should surgery be needed.

It is clear that being overweight is unhealthy. But how can we know whether a person is overweight? And if someone is overweight, what can that person do to lose excess weight? The experiments that follow will help you answer those and other important questions.

4.1 What Is Happening to Your Weight?

Materials:
-scale to measure your weight

To see if your weight is changing, you can weigh yourself and record your weight in your science notebook each day for at least a month. To be consistent, weigh yourself at the same time each day. To see why, record your weight before and after eating a large meal. What happened to your weight after eating? Design and carry out an experiment to find out whether your weight changes while you sleep. If it does, can you explain why?

After a month of daily weighings, has your weight changed? If you gained weight, it may be because you are growing. If you think you are growing, have a parent carefully measure your height. Record the result and then make another measurement after another month of daily weighings. Are you growing taller as well as heavier?

What happens to your weight during spirited exercise? To find out, weigh yourself before and immediately after you have engaged in a vigorous workout for an hour or more. What happened to your weight during exercise? Can you explain why?

In the next activity you will discover objective ways to determine whether a person is underweight, overweight, or even obese.

Science Fair Project Ideas

- Survey friends and family on their use of artificial sweeteners. Compare the Calories "saved" by the sweeteners and make graphs to show what the daily Caloric intake would be if sugar were used in their place. Research the safety of artificial sweeteners and find out what researchers have discovered about their effect on weight control.

- Determine the amount of each nutrient you consume during one week. You can weigh the food used each day and calculate the nutrient amounts using tables that contain percentages of nutrients in different foods. How does the result compare with the daily value calculated from nutritional labels?

Materials:
-Tables 6 and 7
-calculator (optional)

Experts estimate that more than half of all Americans are overweight, and one in every four adults is obese; that is, excessively fat.

Deciding whether you are overweight is not easy. However, there are objective ways to make such judgments. One way is to use the "body mass index," or BMI.

CALCULATING BMI

To find your BMI, divide your weight in pounds by the square of your height in inches, then multiply by 703. The formula for finding a person's BMI is

$$\frac{W}{h^2} \times 703 = BMI.$$

W stands for the person's weight, in pounds, and h represents the person's height, in inches. For example, suppose a fifteen-year-old girl was 5 feet (60 in) tall and weighed 100 pounds. Her BMI is 19.5, determined by the following formula.

$$\frac{100}{60 \times 60} \times 703 = 19.5$$

What does a BMI of 19.5 mean? A person's age determines which chart to use to interpret this BMI. For children and teens under twenty years old, the chart on page 75 or 77 is used. This chart comes from the Centers for Disease Control and Prevention (CDC). For adults twenty years old or older, BMI is interpreted using Table 6. To interpret the BMI of 19.5 for the fifteen-year-old girl, look at the chart for girls (p. 75). Her data puts her between the 25th and 50th percentiles (represented by the blue dot). The key tells us this is a healthy weight.

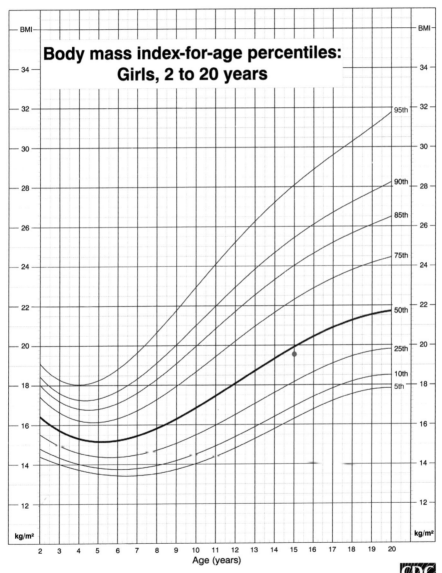

CDC Growth Charts: United States

Body mass index-for-age percentiles: Girls, 2 to 20 years

Published May 30, 2000.
SOURCE: Developed by the National Center for Health Statistics in collaboration with the National Center for Chronic Disease Prevention and Health Promotion (2000).

As Table 6 indicates, a BMI between 18.5 and 25 is regarded as normal for people twenty and older.

TABLE 6.

Weight Status and BMI Ranges for Adults, Twenty Years Old and Older

BMI	Weight Status
Below 18.5	Underweight
18.5 – 24.9	Normal
25.0 – 29.9	Overweight
30.0 and Above	Obese

What is your BMI? Are you considered normal, overweight, or underweight? What are the BMIs of the members of your family? Of friends and classmates? Be sure to explain what you intend to do before asking any volunteers for the information needed to calculate their BMI. Some people are very sensitive about their weight, particularly if they are overweight or underweight.

There are cases where a BMI can be misleading. For example, a professional football player might be 72 inches tall and weigh 240 pounds. What is his BMI?

BMI is a valid indicator for most people, but muscular people or highly trained athletes may be exceptions. Despite a BMI that indicates an overweight condition, the player's muscles and ability to run 100 yards in 10 seconds indicate that he is in better physical condition than

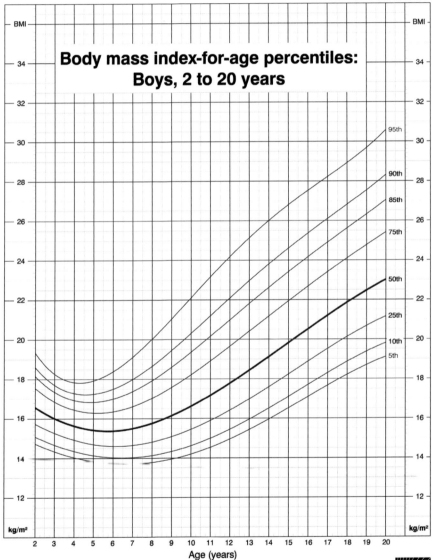

CDC Growth Charts: United States

Body mass index-for-age percentiles: Boys, 2 to 20 years

Published May 30, 2000.
SOURCE: Developed by the National Center for Health Statistics in collaboration with
the National Center for Chronic Disease Prevention and Health Promotion (2000).

CDC
SAFER · HEALTHIER · PEOPLE™

most people. For such people, a better indicator is the percentage of fat in their bodies, which can be determined by finding their lean body weight (LBW).

USING THE PINCH TEST

There is more to good health than a normal weight. As much of that weight as possible should be lean weight—muscle, not fat. You can have a normal BMI and still be flabby. To build or maintain muscle cells you have to exercise. Everyone who is healthy should exercise at least 30 minutes each day. Even a daily walk at 3 to 4 miles per hour for half an hour each day will help, but an hour or more of vigorous exercise is better.

A quick way to determine if a person is too fat is the pinch test. Simply pinch the flesh on the back of the arm as the arm hangs at the side of the body. If the flesh is an inch or more thick, the person is probably overweight.

Have someone apply the pinch test to you. What does it indicate?

An accurate determination of the percentage of fat in a human body can be obtained by weighing the individual in water, determining the body's volume, and calculating the density. Knowing the density of fat and nonfat tissue, the individual's fat content can be determined.

ATTAINING A PROPER BMI THROUGH DIETING

To attain a BMI between 19 and 25 and a lean or normal body in terms of percentage of body fat, you need to exercise. Without exercise you cannot build the muscle cells that make for a lean body. By participating in sports, not riding when you can walk, not taking an elevator when you can climb stairs, and finding a job that requires physical effort, you can get the exercise you need.

At the same time, you should avoid eating large quantities of food or foods with a high-Calorie content. Also, stay away from snacks and sweets, such as candy. If the feeling of hunger becomes intense between meals, eat raw vegetables and fruit or drink fruit juice. Eat only meals served at a table; don't eat in front of the TV. If you are overweight, obtain a diet from your doctor and eat only those foods in the prescribed amounts that appear on the diet.

Maintaining a proper diet is not an easy task. You do have to eat. Fasting (not eating) or bulimia (regurgitating food before it can be digested) can lead to weight loss—but such methods are dangerous because they prevent essential vitamins, minerals, and proteins from reaching the body's cells. People who are overweight need to eat food that provides all the essential nutrients while limiting the Caloric content of food to an amount less than the energy they expend. As long as the body's energy intake is less than its energy output, weight will be lost. The body will draw the extra energy it needs from fat stored in adipose tissue.

MyPyramid shown in Figure 10 in Chapter 3 is an attempt to show the relative quantities of the six basic types of food that you should eat. The colors orange, red, yellow, blue, and purple represent the five different food groups. Small amounts of oils are also needed. The different stripe sizes remind you to choose more foods from the food groups with the widest stripes. From MyPyramid you can see that a nutritious 1,800-Calorie diet should follow rules similar to those listed below. (You can also go to MyPyramid.gov to find the amounts that are right for you.)

- Eat 6 ounces of grains every day, at least half of which should be whole grains.
- Eat 2½ cups of brightly colored vegetables, such as broccoli, spinach, carrots or sweet potatoes.
- Eat 1½ cups of fruit but go easy on juice. Make sure the juice you drink is 100 percent juice.
- Drink or eat 3 cups of lowfat or fat-free milk, yogurt, or cheese in order to get your calcium.

- Eat 5 ounces of lean or lowfat meat, chicken, turkey, and fish. Ask for it baked, broiled, or grilled—not fried. Nuts, seeds, peas, and beans are great sources of protein, too.
- Oils are not a food group, but you need some for good health. Get your oils from fish, nuts, and liquid oils such as olive oil, corn oil, soybean oil, and canola oil.
- Limit your intake of fats and sugars. Use Nutritional Facts labels and limit solid fats as well as foods that contain them. Choose food and beverages low in added sugars and other Caloric sweeteners.

In addition to providing guidelines for a healthy diet, MyPyramid also reminds you to be physically active. Did you notice a person climbing the stairs of the pyramid? You should aim for at least 60 minutes of activity every day or most days. Walk, run, dance, swim, bike, rollerblade—it all counts. How great is that!

 Science Fair Project Idea

Pick two people of very different ages. Ask them to write down what they eat and their schedule, including daily exercise and activities for a week. With this data, calculate the Calories that they eat and burn. Relate their diets to their gender, age, height, and weight.

Materials:

- cartons of skim (fat-free), 1 percent, 2 percent, and whole milk
- 10 small, clear plastic vials
- labels
- marking pen
- eyedroppers
- hot and cold tap water
- food coloring

Half a century ago milk came in clear glass, one-quart bottles. You could see the yellowish cream (the fatty part of the milk) at the top of the bottle. Because the fat was less dense than the rest of the milk, it would float on the whiter milk in the lower part of the bottle. If you wanted milk with less fat, you could pour off the cream. Many farm families poured milk into large pans and let the cream rise to the surface. They then skimmed the cream from the surface and churned it into butter.

Today most milk comes in quart, half-gallon, or gallon containers made of plastic or cardboard. You can buy whole milk, which still has the cream in it; skim milk, from which all the cream has been removed; or "percentage" milks from which only some of the cream has been removed. The cream in whole milk is not visible because it has been homogenized—that is, broken into tiny particles that stay suspended in the rest of the milk.

VOLUME CONVERSIONS YOU MAY NEED

There are 8 fluid ounces in a cup, 4 cups in a quart, and 4 quarts in a gallon. How many ounces are in a quart? In a gallon?

How many cups of milk fill a gallon jug?

A gallon is the same volume as 3.785 liters (l). How many cups are in one liter? How many fluid ounces are in one liter? How many milliliters (ml) are in one fluid ounce?

In most stores, you can buy skim (fat-free) milk, 1 percent fat milk, 2 percent fat milk, and whole milk. Milk has a density that is approximately the same as that of water, 1.0 gram per milliliter (1.0 g/ml). This means that each milliliter (ml) or cubic centimeter (cm^3) of milk weighs approximately 1.0 g.

A quart of milk contains 946 ml. How many grams of fat are in a quart of 1 percent milk? In a quart of 2 percent milk? In a quart of skim milk?

A cup of milk is 1/4 of a quart. How many milliliters are in a cup of milk? How much fat, in grams, is present in a cup of 1 percent milk? In a cup of 2 percent milk? In a cup of whole milk? In a gallon of whole milk?

Examine the nutritional facts on the labels of each kind of milk. How does the percentage of fat in milk affect its sodium content? Its sugar content? Its protein content? Its fiber content? Its mineral content? Its cholesterol content?

How much fortified milk should you drink each day to obtain your daily requirement of vitamin A? Of vitamin C? Of vitamin D? Of calcium? Does the percentage of fat in milk affect the ratio of total fat to saturated fat? What nutrition facts change when you buy fortified milk?

MILK AND WATER DENSITIES

Earlier you read that the density of milk is approximately the same as the density of water; that is, each milliliter weighs approximately 1.0 g. To see whether the density of milk is slightly more, slightly less, or equal to the density of water, you can do a simple experiment. Place small samples of whole, 2 percent, 1 percent, and fat-free milk in small, clear plastic vials. Label the vials so you can identify each milk sample. Nearly fill an equal number of vials with tap water. Place them near the samples of milk.

Leave the liquids for about an hour so that they all reach room temperature.

Now you are ready to compare densities. With an eyedropper remove some whole milk from its vial. Carefully place the tip of the eyedropper in the center of a vial of water, as shown in Figure 13. *Very gently* squeeze the bulb of the eyedropper so that a small amount of milk emerges from the end of the eyedropper. Does the drop of milk fall, ascend, or remain in place as it comes out of the eyedropper into the water? What does this tell you about its density as compared to the density of water?

Repeat the experiment with clean eyedroppers using 2 percent, 1 percent, and fat-free milk. How does the density of each milk sample compare with the density of water?

[FIGURE 13]

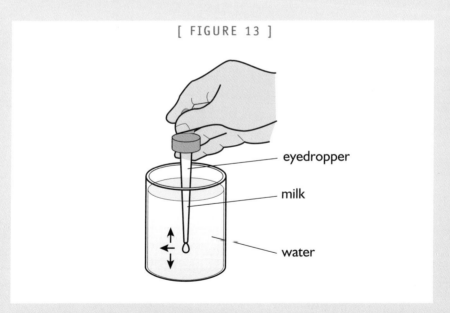

eyedropper

milk

water

What happens when you gently squeeze a drop of milk into clear water? Does the drop sink, rise to the surface, or remain in the middle of the water?

To see why the temperatures of the milk and water should be the same, pour some cold tap water into a clear vial. Using a clean eyedropper, add a drop or two of food coloring to a second vial before you fill it with hot tap water. Remove some of the colored hot water with another clean eyedropper. Carefully place the end of the eyedropper in the cold water and *very gently* squeeze a little of the colored hot water into the center of the cold water. Does the colored hot water sink or rise in the cold water?

Repeat the experiment, but this time add food coloring to the cold water. If you gently squeeze a drop or two of the colored cold water into a vial of colorless hot water, do you think the cold water will sink or rise in the hot water? Try it! Were you right?

 Science Fair Project Ideas

- Design and carry out an experiment to compare the actual densities, in grams per milliliter, of milk with different fat percentages. What do you find?
- To prepare milk without fat, farmers used to let the cream (the fatty part of the milk) rise to the surface of the milk. They would then skim off the cream. Hence the name "skim milk." How do modern dairies control the amount of fat in the milk they sell?

4.4 What is the Nutritional Value of Milk and a Hot Dog?

Materials:

- 2 percent milk
- package of beef hot dogs
- package of hot dog rolls
- calculator (optional)

Suppose you decide to have a glass of 2 percent milk and a beef hot dog with a roll. Read the labels on all three foods. How many Calories are provided by the milk? By the hot dog? By the roll? What percentage of the Calories from each food are from fat? What is the total number of Calories from fat? What percentage of the Calories in this simple meal are from fat?

How much calcium will you obtain from the milk? From the hot dog? From the roll?

Would you consider a glass of milk, a hot dog, and a roll a nutritious meal? Explain why or why not.

Science Fair Project Ideas

- Choose two or more different brands of hot dogs. Compare and contrast fat content and nutritional value of the different brands.

- Hot dogs are served with a variety of condiments such as ketchup, mustard, relish, and others. Find out the nutritional value of some different condiments. Which ones add nutritional value to the meal?

- Use the Internet to learn more about saturated, unsaturated, polyunsaturated, and monounsaturated fats. How do they differ? Which poses greater health risks?

4.5 How Many Calories Does One Potato Chip Contain?

Materials:

- an adult
- large metal can
- metal shears
- hammer
- large nail
- aluminum foil
- water
- measuring cup
- metric ruler
- matches
- household thermometer
- baby food jars
- potato chips

Your favorite aisles at a supermarket are likely the ones with the snack foods, desserts, and candies. In fact, these aisles are probably the favorite ones for many people. Most people can recall days when they devoured a large container of popcorn at the movies, downed a whole bag of pretzels at a picnic, or ate a bowl of potato chips while watching television. Although these snack foods may satisfy our hunger, they provide only limited quantities of important nutrients. Moreover, if a person maintained a steady diet of these foods, the extra pounds would quickly begin to show. The same is true not only of snack foods but also of desserts and candies. The increased weight would result from the large number of Calories present in these foods. One snack food that contains a lot of calories, no matter how you spell it, is a potato chip.

The first potato chip came about as a result of a practical joke. In 1854, a wealthy American named Cornelius Vanderbilt was dining at a restaurant in Saratoga Springs, New York. When his meal was served, he was not happy with the way his fried potatoes looked. He thought they were too thick and ordered the waiter to take them back to the kitchen.

[FIGURE 14]

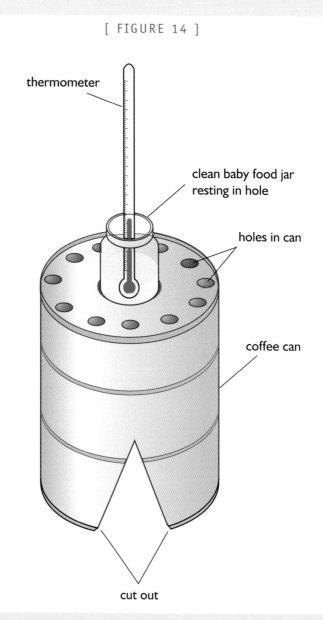

thermometer

clean baby food jar
resting in hole

holes in can

coffee can

cut out

You can use a large metal can to construct a calorimeter. As the food sample underneath the glass jar burns, the temperature of the water inside the jar rises. Why would wrapping the metal can and the glass jar in aluminum foil be a good idea?

The chef was annoyed and decided to retaliate. He cut paper-thin slices of potatoes and then fried them to a crisp in hot oil. Little did the chef suspect what would happen next. When he was served his fried potatoes this time, Vanderbilt loved them. Potato chips had been created and would soon become a huge success. Now that you know how potato chips were first made, the next time you open a bag, save a few for an experiment. In that way, you will also save a few Calories.

Use a large metal can to construct a calorimeter, a device for measuring the energy in foods as shown in Figure 14. A coffee can or any other large, metal container is suitable. Remove the top. **Ask an adult** to use metal shears to cut out a wedge along one edge. Invert the can so that the bottom is upright. Carefully cut a hole in the bottom, wide enough to hold a small baby food jar. Be sure that the hole is large enough to hold the jar but not so large that the jar falls through the hole. If you have made the hole too large, wrap the jar with aluminum foil to get a tight fit. **Ask an adult** to use a hammer and a large nail to punch several air holes around this opening.

Place the baby food jar in the hole. Pour 30 ml (approximately 1 fluid ounce) of water into the jar. Place a thermometer into the jar and record the water temperature. Then make a small "frying pan" out of a sheet of aluminum foil. Place the potato chip in the frying pan. You will have to rig up something so that the potato chip rests about 2 cm (1 in) below the bottom of the baby food jar in the can. You might place the frying pan with its potato chip on another baby food jar or a small glass.

Remove your calorimeter and ask an adult to ignite the potato chip with a match. The chip should burn fairly easily because of the oils it contains, but your helper may have to try lighting it more than once. If your potato chip does not ignite, try another one. Once the chip is burning, carefully place your calorimeter over it. Be sure that the bottom of the baby food jar does not extinguish the flame. After the potato chip has burned completely, observe the thermometer and record the highest temperature of the water.

As the potato chip burns, heat energy is transferred to the water. To calculate the number of calories (not Calories) in the chip, place your data into the following equation:

$$\text{calories} = \text{volume of water} \times (\text{final water temperature} - \text{initial water temperature})$$

For example, if the temperature of the water inside the baby jar went from 22°C to 68°C, then you would get the following result:

$$\text{calories} = 30 \times (68-22) = 30 \times 46 = 1{,}380 \text{ calories (or 1.38 Calories)}$$

Notice that the formula uses volume of water, while calorie was defined in terms of the mass of water that is used in the calorimeter. At most temperatures, 1 g of water equals approximately 1 ml of water. Thus, you can substitute the volume of water in the equation for calculating calories, but the volume must be in milliliters (ml). If your measuring device is marked in fluid ounces, then use the following formula to convert:

$$946 \text{ ml} = 32 \text{ fluid ounces}$$

How many calories did your potato chip contain? How many Calories? Check a reference source in your school library or on the Internet to see how many calories are recommended daily for someone your age, gender, height, weight, and degree of activity. How many potato chips would you have to eat in a day to obtain that number of calories? You can repeat this experiment, this time using a peanut or a walnut to determine its calorie content. No matter what you use, why is your calorimeter not as accurate as it could be? To determine the actual calorie content of a food sample, scientists use an insulated calorimeter where an electrical discharge ignites the food sample. What advantages does such a calorimeter have over the one you used?

By the way, you may have noticed a green or brown potato chip when you took one from the bag for your experiment. A brown chip has not been "over-fried" or burned by the manufacturer. Rather a brown chip comes from a potato that contains more sugar. The more sugar in a chip, the browner it gets when it is fried. A green chip is from a potato that has been exposed to the sun. Normally, potatoes grow underground, but strong winds and heavy rains can erode the soil, exposing a potato to the sun. Like all plants, a potato produces the green pigment chlorophyll when exposed to sunlight.

Science Fair Project Ideas

- Potato chips contain a substance called acrylamide. It is produced when certain foods (such as potatoes) are cooked at high temperatures in processes such as frying, baking, or roasting. Check the Internet for information about acrylamide. In what other foods does acrylamide form? Are there health risks associated with its consumption?

- One of the major problems facing the snack food industry has always been how to make a product that is nutritious, nonfattening, and tasty. After years of research, an artificial chemical compound called olestra, known commercially as Olean, was developed. In 1996, Olean was approved for use in certain snack foods by the Food and Drug Administration. Tests showed that very few people could tell the difference between regular potato chips and those containing Olean. Chips with Olean, however, contain half the Calories of regular chips. Moreover, Olean chips do not have any fat. Check the Internet for information about Olean. How is it made? What side effects have people experienced after eating potato chips made with Olean? How widely is it currently used?

Materials:

- yeast
- measuring cup
- tablespoon
- measuring teaspoons
- 6 small plastic freezer bags
- water
- sugar
- flour
- cookies
- wax paper
- rolling pin
- marking pen

Many people eat milk and cookies at lunchtime, so you should not have any trouble getting a variety of cookies to use in this experiment. But then again, your friends are not likely to give up their cookies unless you are very persuasive. Tell them that their cookies will be put to good use. Inform them that you need the cookies to tell which brand contains the least amount of sugar.

Use a marker to number 6 plastic freezer bags. Place 1 tablespoon of yeast and ¼ cup of water in freezer bag #1. Stand the bag upright so that the contents do not spill but do not seal the bag. Do the same to 5 other bags. Bag #1 will serve as the control.

Add 1/4 teaspoon of sugar to bag #2, ½ teaspoon of sugar to bag #3, and 1 teaspoon of sugar to bag #4. Add 1 tablespoon of flour to bag #5. Use a rolling pin to gently crush a cookie between two sheets of wax paper. Add 1 tablespoon of cookie crumbs to bag #6. Check each bag against Figure 15, which shows what should be in each bag.

Squeeze out all the air from each bag and seal. Mix the contents thoroughly. Allow the bags to remain undisturbed for 30 minutes. Observe what happens.

The sugar reacts with an enzyme supplied by the yeast. The reaction produces carbon dioxide gas, which inflates the freezer bag. The more carbon dioxide produced, the bigger the bag gets. By comparing the size of the bag with the crushed cookie to those containing sugar, you can estimate how much sugar is present in 1 tablespoon of crushed cookie. You can test as many different brands of cookies as you want, depending on how convincing you were to your lunchtime friends. By the way, why did you crush the cookie?

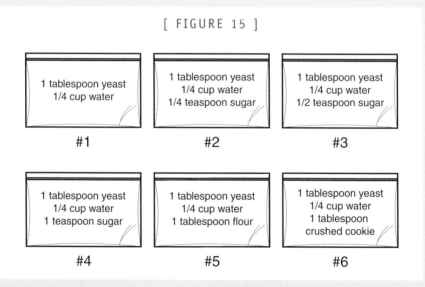

[FIGURE 15]

1 tablespoon yeast
1/4 cup water

#1

1 tablespoon yeast
1/4 cup water
1/4 teaspoon sugar

#2

1 tablespoon yeast
1/4 cup water
1/2 teaspoon sugar

#3

1 tablespoon yeast
1/4 cup water
1 teaspoon sugar

#4

1 tablespoon yeast
1/4 cup water
1 tablespoon flour

#5

1 tablespoon yeast
1/4 cup water
1 tablespoon
crushed cookie

#6

Check your bags against the bags shown here to be sure that you have placed the correct ingredients in each bag.

Science Fair Project Ideas

- Investigate the great variety of diets described in books and magazine articles. These might include high-protein, high-fat, low-carbohydrate, and one-food diets, as well as diet pills and diuretics. Write criticisms of these diets and discuss your analysis with a nutritionist.

- Plan menus for your family for a week. Estimate the amount of nutrients and the cost. Suggest how the diet of your family might be improved without any great increase in cost.

- Collect daily food diaries from a large number of family members, friends, or classmates. Compare them to the food pyramid and make bar graphs to show how many people meet the guidelines for the various food groups.

Chapter 5

Vitamins and Other Health Products

YOU ARE PROBABLY FAMILIAR WITH A WIDE VARIETY OF PRODUCTS THAT ENHANCE HEALTH. They may be related to your diet, such as vitamins and mineral supplements, which, in some cases, can help prevent disease. Some products may be used when you are outdoors taking part in the physical activities so vital to good health and fitness. Suncreens and sunblocks prevent certain types of ultraviolet rays from damaging your skin. You may get scrapes or abrasions playing sports and require antibiotic cream to prevent infection. Other products you or your family members and friends use to maintain good health are related to personal hygiene or cleaning your body. They include soaps, toothpaste, and shampoo. These products remove bacteria from your body. In this chapter, you will conduct experiments to learn more about these products.

In 1781 a regiment of about eight hundred British soldiers sailed for India. After nearly a year at sea, the soldiers finally reached their destination. By that time, 121 soldiers had died from a disease called *scurvy*. The first visible sign of scurvy is red spots that appear on the legs, arms, and back. A person with scurvy soon becomes weak and develops pain in the joints. Internal bleeding produces black-and-blue marks. The gums become so soft that teeth easily fall out. Eating becomes difficult and painful.

In 1747 a British doctor named James Lind studied twelve people who had scurvy. He divided the twelve people evenly into two groups—a control group and an experimental group. Those in the experimental group were given lemons and oranges to eat. Those six people recovered from scurvy. However, the six people in the control group were not given fruit, and they did not recover.

Lind later discovered that limes were just as effective as lemons and oranges in preventing scurvy. He seemed to have found the cure for this disease—35 years before the deaths of those 121 British soldiers and thousands of others on long sea voyages. However, it took Lind 41 years to convince the British Royal Navy that he had found a cure for scurvy. In 1795 the British Royal Navy finally required that all its sailors drink some lime juice every day. For that reason, British sailors became known as limeys.

In the 1880s a Japanese doctor named Kanehiro Takaki was investigating another disease. Takaki was trying to find out why almost half of Japanese sailors were developing *beriberi*. The first sign of beriberi is overall weakness, followed by a loss of feeling in the feet and legs. The body then swells up because fluids collect inside. If a person does not recover from beriberi, the heart may stop working.

Takaki observed that Japanese sailors were eating mostly rice in their daily rations. He found that replacing some of the rice with vegetables, fish, and meat prevented beriberi. Soon after Takaki's findings, the Japanese Navy required that all its sailors follow his diet. In six years, beriberi was no longer a health threat to Japanese sailors.

In 1913 Joseph Goldberger began to investigate the cause of still another disease. Known as *pellagra*, this disease was quickly becoming an epidemic in several southern U.S. states. Pellagra causes skin rashes, mouth sores, and diarrhea. If a person does not recover, pellagra can affect the brain. Goldberger investigated the cause of pellagra by working with inmates who were serving time for minor crimes in a Mississippi prison. Those who volunteered to take part in his experiment would get a pardon.

Half the prison volunteers made up the control group. Those inmates continued to eat the usual prison food, which was well balanced. The other half in the experimental group were given a diet that was typical of what poor people in the South were eating—cornbread, molasses, and a little pork fat. Within months, those in the experimental group developed pellagra. The symptoms of the disease disappeared when the inmates were given meat, fresh vegetables, and milk.

What all these studies had shown was the value of eating the right foods. What Lind, Takaki, and Goldberger did not know was that the right foods contain substances, called vitamins, that the body needs to stay healthy. Without those substances called vitamins, diseases such as scurvy (lack of vitamin C), beriberi (lack of vitamin B1, or thiamin), and pellagra (lack of niacin) may set in. A well-balanced diet should provide all the vitamins the body needs to stay healthy. Today, vitamin supplements are only one of the health care products that people regularly use.

Materials:
- measuring cup
- water
- large glass jar
- spray starch
- Lugol's solution (borrowed from your science teacher)
- eyedropper
- small glass jar
- vitamin C tablet
- wax paper
- large spoon or small hammer
- orange juice

Many people do not make the effort to eat foods that supply enough of the vitamins they need. They sometimes rely on fast or processed foods that provide little, if any, nutritional value. Moreover, fresh vegetables that have been stored too long or overcooked contain greatly reduced amounts of vitamins. To make up for the loss of vitamins in their food, more and more people are taking vitamin supplements on a regular basis.

One vitamin that many people take in large doses is vitamin C. The scientific name for vitamin C is ascorbic acid. Vitamin C is required for healthy bones and gums. It is also needed for the growth and repair of body tissues. One consequence of not getting enough vitamin C is scurvy.

An alternative to taking vitamin C tablets is to drink fruit juices and to eat citrus fruits, such as lemons, oranges, and limes. These juices and fruits are rich in vitamin C. This experiment will show you how to find out which brand of orange juice contains the most vitamin C.

Pour 1 cup of cold water into a large glass jar. Squirt some spray starch into the water. Swirl gently to dissolve the starch. Add 10 drops of Lugol's solution. Many biology or life science classrooms have Lugol's solution for staining specimens to view under a microscope. Ask a science teacher for a small bottle. Be careful not to spill the Lugol's solution, as it will stain your hands and clothes. The color of the starch solution should be royal blue. If it is not, add more Lugol's solution.

Pour 30 ml or 1 fluid ounce of the starch-iodine solution into a small glass jar. To see what happens when vitamin C is added to this

[FIGURE 16]

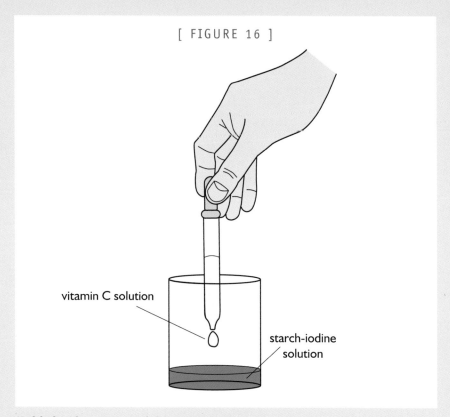

vitamin C solution

starch-iodine solution

Hold the dropper straight up and down. In this way, the drops will all be about the same size. Swirl the starch-iodine solution after adding each drop.

solution, fold a vitamin C tablet inside a piece of wax paper. Crush it by pressing down with a large spoon or small hammer. Dissolve the crushed vitamin C in 1 cup of water. Add a drop of the vitamin C solution to the starch-iodine solution, as shown in Figure 16. Gently swirl the liquids so that they mix thoroughly. Continue adding the vitamin C solution drop by drop until the starch-iodine solution turns from royal blue to colorless. Be sure that you swirl the starch solution after adding each drop.

Lugol's solution combines with starch to form a royal blue color. Vitamin C, however, has a greater attraction than starch for Lugol's solution. Vitamin C combines with Lugol's solution to produce a colorless solution. As you continue to add drops of vitamin C solution, more and more Lugol's solution is removed from the starch. Once all the Lugol's solution has been stripped from the starch, the solution becomes colorless.

Now check to see if your orange juice has vitamin C. Thoroughly clean the glass jar and again add 30 ml (1 fluid ounce) of the starch-iodine solution. This time, add the orange juice, drop by drop, until the starch solution turns colorless. If the juice does not contain any vitamin C, then the starch solution will not turn colorless. Rather the solution will begin to take on the color of the juice. In this case, you can say that the juice did not contain any measurable amount of vitamin C.

By counting the number of drops of juice that you add, you can compare different brands of orange juice to determine which one has the most vitamin C. The less juice you add to turn the starch-iodine solution colorless, the more vitamin C it contains. You can also check out other juices and fresh fruits and vegetables for their vitamin C content. But first you will have to squeeze the juice from the fruits or liquefy them in a blender.

Science Fair Project Ideas

- Vitamin C is not very stable. In other words, vitamin C breaks down easily. Design an experiment to test how temperature, light, and exposure to the air affect the vitamin content of a food or supplement. You can use either a solution prepared with a vitamin C tablet or a juice that you find contains a high vitamin C concentration. Check out whether both cooling and heating cause vitamin C to break down. Is there one temperature at which vitamin C is most stable? When testing the effect of light on the stability of vitamin C, be sure to vary the amount of light to which the juice or solution is exposed. Check out whether all types of light (incandescent, fluorescent, halogen, or sun) produce the same results.

- It's easier to overdose on a fat-soluble vitamin than on a water-soluble one. That's because any excess of a water-soluble vitamin, such as vitamin C or vitamin B, dissolves in the watery part of blood called the plasma. The vitamins travel through the bloodstream to the kidneys, where they are eliminated from the body. In contrast, fat-soluble vitamins are stored in the fat of the liver. Over time, stored vitamins may cause fat deposits to build up in the liver and

(continued on next page)

(continued from previous page)

interfere with its functions.

Fat-soluble vitamins, such as vitamin A, are present in foods in only small amounts. Thus, it is usually impossible to consume too much of these vitamins. However, some people take large quantities of vitamin tablets on a daily basis. Large doses of fat-soluble vitamins, if taken over a long time, can overload the liver and cause health problems. For example, large doses of vitamin A can reduce the density of bones, leading to a disease called osteoporosis. Design a project to alert consumers about the dangers of taking too many fat-soluble vitamins. Do research to find information about each vitamin and its possible effect on a person's health if taken in large quantities for too long.

- Design an experiment to test if a vitamin has some adverse affect on a living creature other than a human or other vertebrate. For example, you can investigate the vitamin's effect on a freshwater flatworm called a planarian, which is shown in Figure 17. These animals have an amazing ability to regenerate lost parts. Your project can investigate whether high doses of a fat-soluble vitamin affect their ability to regenerate. But first you must work out a way of getting the fat-soluble vitamin to dissolve in the water. You could dissolve the vitamin in vegetable oil, then use a liquid soap to disperse the oil in water, but be sure to set up the proper control to see if soap or oil alone has any effect on regeneration.

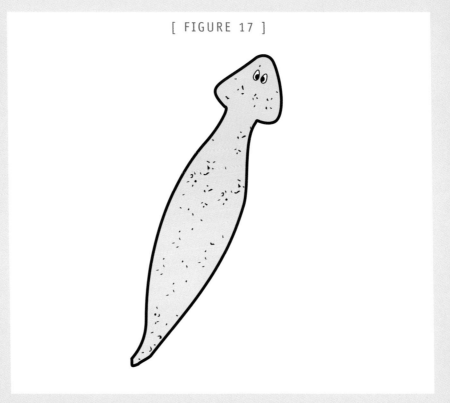

[FIGURE 17]

A planarian, a freshwater flatworm, can be used to see if large doses of vitamins affect its ability to regenerate lost parts.

Materials:
- sunlight
- scissors
- newspaper
- white construction paper
- stapler
- marking pen
- labels
- 3 resealable plastic bags
- 2 sunscreen products (one with an SPF rating twice that of the other)

The rays from the sun that can damage skin are called *ultraviolet (UV) radiation*. UV exists in two forms that affect the skin: ultraviolet-A (UVA) and ultraviolet-B (UVB). UVB is more powerful than UVA in producing a sunburn. UVB is also a cause of several types of skin cancer.

Sunscreens contain numerous ingredients. Some ingredients reflect or scatter ultraviolet radiation. Other ingredients absorb UV radiation, dissipating it as heat. Some sunscreens protect against both UVA and UVB, but some only prevent UVB radiation from penetrating deep into the skin to cause sunburn. Sunscreens are rated for how much protection they provide against UVB. This rating is known as the *sun protection factor*, or SPF. The label on a sunscreen product indicates its SPF rating.

The SPF indicates the amount of protection offered against skin-reddening from UVB compared to the time it takes for the skin to redden without sunscreen protection. The amount of time it takes for a person to begin reddening without protection is known as the *minimal erythmal dose*, or MED. Assume that a person's MED is 10 minutes. Using a sunscreen with an SPF of 15 extends time in the sun without a burn for 15 times 10 minutes, or 150 minutes. A sunscreen with an SPF rating of 30 allows the person to remain in the sun for 30 times 10 minutes, or 300 minutes, without burning.

That's five hours, or about the same as a full day at the beach, but such a long time in the sun is still unsafe, even with sunscreen. Why? Because the SPF does not indicate how much UVA protection the sunscreen provides. Although UVA is less likely than UVB to cause sunburn, UVA may be responsible for as many as 90 percent of the *melanomas*, a particularly lethal form of skin cancer. Thus, sunscreens prevent sunburns but, over time, exposure to the sun's rays can still cause skin cancer, no matter how much sunscreen is applied. To provide greater UVA protection, experts recommend purchasing a sunscreen labeled "broad-spectrum."

This experiment will allow you to test whether a sunscreen with an SPF rating twice that of another sunscreen is really twice as effective in absorbing ultraviolet light. Rather than testing how quickly skin reddens, you will evaluate how quickly newspaper yellows because of exposure to ultraviolet light.

Cut three equal-sized strips of newspaper and three slightly larger strips of white construction paper small enough to fit inside three resealable plastic bags. To keep the newspaper flat, staple the ends of each strip to a piece of construction paper. Place one sample in each of the three plastic bags and seal. Label the bags A, B, and C. Figure 18 shows how to make sure that the samples do not slide around when you move the plastic bags.

Apply a layer of one sunscreen to the outside of bag A, directly over the newspaper strip. Apply a layer of the other sunscreen to the outside of bag B, again directly over the newspaper strip. Bag C will have no sunscreen and serve as the control. Place the three bags in direct sunlight. Ultraviolet rays from the sun cause newspaper to turn yellow. Note how long it takes for each newspaper strip to start turning yellow. Obviously, the control should yellow first.

How does the sunscreen with twice the SPF rating stack up against the other sunscreen?

You can expand this experiment to check out sunscreens with different SPF ratings. You can also compare expensive versus inexpensive brands with the same SPF ratings to see if the extra cost is justified. Of course, some sunscreens feel like rubber on your skin, while others let your skin breathe.

[FIGURE 18]

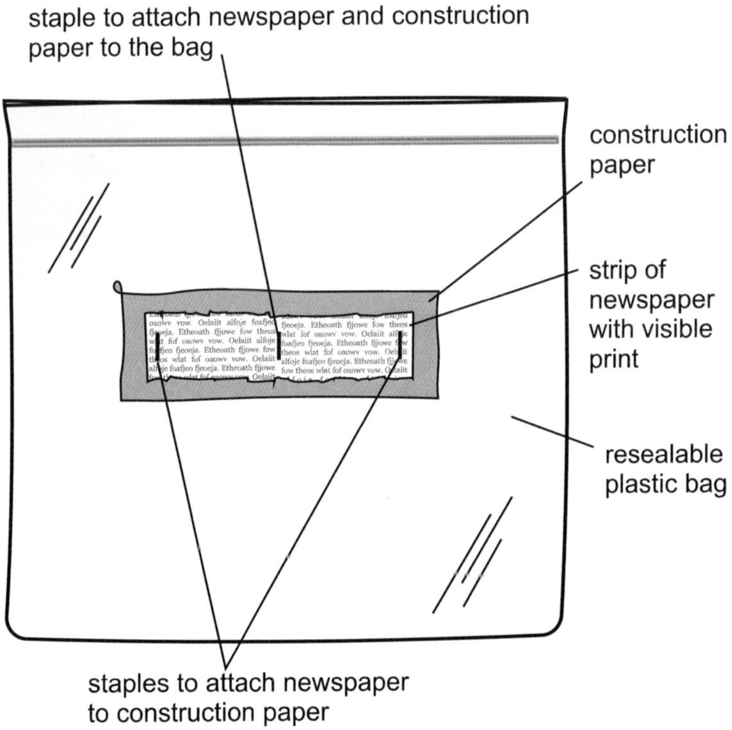

staple to attach newspaper and construction paper to the bag

construction paper

strip of newspaper with visible print

resealable plastic bag

staples to attach newspaper to construction paper

Staple each newspaper strip to a strip of construction paper to keep the newspaper flat. Then place one strip in each of the three bags and seal. Staple once through the bag so that the strip is held in place in each bag.

Science Fair Project Idea

Sunblocks such as zinc oxide are white creams that remain clearly visible after they are applied to the skin. Sunscreens are invisible. Design an experiment to compare the effectiveness of sunblocks and sunscreens using photosensitive paper. You can check with someone who is familiar with photography for advice on how to proceed.

5.3 How Does Antibacterial Cream Affect Bacteria?

Materials:

- an adult
- 2 large metal lids (like those from a mayonnaise jar)
- marking pen
- plain gelatin
- water
- kettle or pot to boil water
- tablespoon
- measuring cup
- sugar
- plastic wrap
- refrigerator
- antibiotic cream
- cotton swab
- pair of rubber kitchen gloves
- pencil
- bleach

Another health care product that you might have at home is antibiotic cream. You or a family member may have applied an antibiotic cream to a cut on your skin. The cream is designed to kill germs before they can enter your body and cause infection. This experiment will give you the chance to evaluate how well an antibiotic cream does its job.

Label the top of one large metal lid A and a second metal lid B. **Ask an adult** to help you dissolve some plain gelatin in boiling water according to the directions on the package. Add a tablespoon of sugar to the liquid. The gelatin will serve as a surface on which bacteria can grow. The sugar will provide the nutrients for the bacteria. Before the gelatin hardens, pour a small amount into each of the two lids. Cover both lids with a piece of plastic wrap. Allow the gelatin to harden in a refrigerator overnight.

The next day, remove the plastic wrap and place a small dab of antibiotic cream on the gelatin in lid A. Use a cotton swab to spread the cream over the surface of the gelatin. Expose the gelatin in both lids to the air for 24 hours. Then seal each lid with plastic wrap. Keep the lids in a warm place. After several days, bacteria that landed on the gelatin will grow and multiply to form colonies, such as those shown in Figure 19.

Each type of bacteria can form a different-looking colony. Each colony represents millions of bacteria that developed from just one or a few bacteria that landed on that spot. Obviously, if the antibiotic cream was effective, then few or even no colonies should grow on lid A.

Bacteria that grow on the gelatin might cause some type of disease. To prevent coming in contact with any of these bacteria, do not touch the gelatin or lid. When you are finished making your observations, put on a pair of rubber kitchen gloves and finish your experiment **under adult supervision**. Use a pencil to poke a hole through the plastic wrap. Pour liquid bleach through the hole to cover the surface of the gelatin. Allow the lids to sit for 24 hours. The bleach will kill the bacteria. Carefully pour off the bleach and thoroughly rinse the lids under running water. Then dispose of the lids properly.

PERSONAL HYGIENE PRODUCTS

Your home undoubtedly contains a wide variety of personal hygiene products to clean your skin, teeth, and hair. Keeping clean is one way to prevent germs from entering the body and causing disease. Germs are living things that are so small they can only be seen with the help of a magnifying lens or a microscope. These very tiny living things are known as *microorganisms*. The prefix *micro* means "very small." An *organism* is any living thing.

Microorganisms were first seen in the mid 1600s by a Dutchman named Antoni van Leeuwenhoek. During his life, Leeuwenhoek made hundreds of glass lenses to study tiny objects. He also examined a variety of liquids, including saliva, blood, and water collected from different sources such as ponds and wells. Leeuwenhoek became the first person to see and describe the miniature world of microorganisms.

However, Leeuwenhoek had no idea that many of the microorganisms he examined could cause disease. In fact, almost two hundred years passed before a connection between microorganisms and disease was discovered. In the 1840s, a Hungarian doctor named Ignaz Semmelweis was working in the maternity ward of a hospital. Semmelweis was shocked to discover that in some cases up to 50 percent of the women died following childbirth.

Semmelweis made an interesting observation. The death rate following childbirth was much higher in the maternity wards where medical students delivered the babies than in those wards where trained women delivered the babies. Semmelweis compared various conditions between the two wards, including bed linens, crowding, ventilation, and the food served. He found them to be the same in both wards. Obviously, none of these conditions could be the cause.

[FIGURE 19]

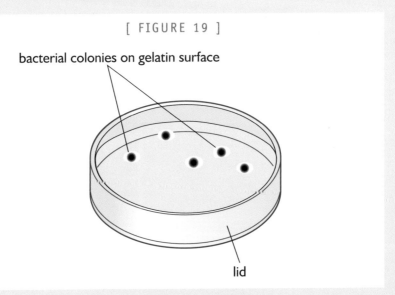

bacterial colonies on gelatin surface

lid

The colonies of bacteria that grow on the gelatin may have different shapes and color. Each represents a different type of bacteria.

Semmelweis then noticed that the medical students rarely washed their hands before delivering a baby. In many cases, these students had just performed an autopsy. Semmelweis believed that the medical students were spreading a disease on their hands to the women who were having babies. He insisted that the medical students scrub their hands with soap and water before delivering a baby. For the first time, the death rate in the maternity wards staffed by medical students dropped below the death rate in the wards staffed by the trained women.

Unfortunately, the value of Semmelweis's work was not immediately recognized. In fact, his superiors at the hospital ridiculed the requirement that medical students wash their hands before delivering a baby. After years of abuse, Semmelweis quit working at the hospital. He died in 1865. The importance of washing with soap to get rid of germs would not be appreciated until several years after his death.

5.4 How Well Does Hand Soap Clean?

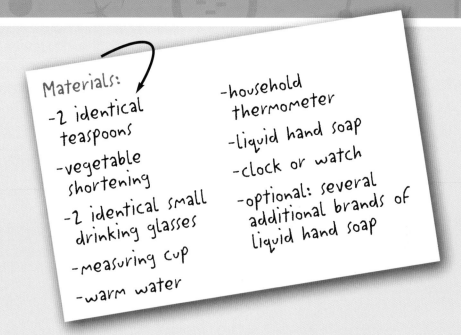

Materials:
- 2 identical teaspoons
- vegetable shortening
- 2 identical small drinking glasses
- measuring cup
- warm water
- household thermometer
- liquid hand soap
- clock or watch
- optional: several additional brands of liquid hand soap

Washing gets rid of the germs and dirt that become trapped in the oils and grease on your skin. If you just wash with water, no matter how hard you scrub, your skin will never get really clean. Oils and grease cannot mix with water, so water alone cannot get rid of the germs and dirt embedded in them. That is why soap is needed.

Think of soap as a lot of people with outstretched arms, with one hand grabbing on to water and the other hand grabbing on to grease. Now imagine what happens when all these people start to move around very quickly. As the people move about, the water and grease mix. The same thing happens when you scrub with soap. One "hand" of soap grabs on to water. The other "hand" grabs on to grease. As you scrub, the soap moves around and mixes the water and grease. The harder you scrub, the cleaner you get because rinsing with water can now wash away the germs and dirt that were trapped in the grease. This experiment will examine how well a hand soap gets rid of grease.

Use your finger to cover both sides of two identical teaspoons with a very light coating of vegetable shortening, as shown in Figure 20.

Vegetable shortening is a grease. Try your best to apply the same amount of shortening to each spoon. Place each spoon in one of two identical small glasses of warm water. Use a measuring cup to be sure that the level of water in each glass is the same. Use a thermometer to be sure that the temperature of the water in each glass is the same.

Add one drop of liquid hand soap to one of the glasses. Gently stir the spoons in both glasses for two minutes. Remove the spoons. Examine them to compare how much shortening is left on each spoon. The spoon stirred in the glass of water that has no soap added is the control.

[FIGURE 20]

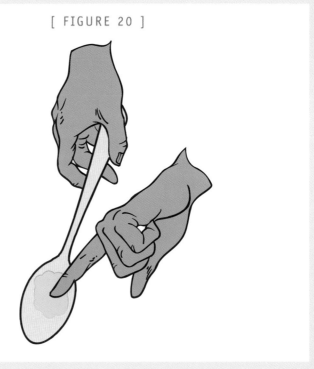

Cover both sides of the bowl of a spoon with a uniform, light coating of vegetable shortening.

Continue adding liquid soap to the first glass, one drop at a time, until all the shortening is removed from the spoon. Stir the spoons for two minutes after adding each drop. How many drops of soap does it take to remove all the shortening?

You can extend this experiment by comparing different brands of soap. The brand that cleans the best is the one that takes the least amount of liquid soap to remove all the shortening from the spoon. Be sure that each experiment you do has only one independent variable—the brand of soap that you are testing. Thus, you must use identical spoons, the same amount of shortening and water, and keep the water temperature the same for all the soap brands you test.

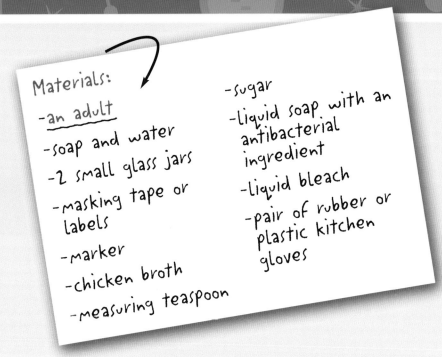

Materials:
- an adult
- soap and water
- 2 small glass jars
- masking tape or labels
- marker
- chicken broth
- measuring teaspoon
- sugar
- liquid soap with an antibacterial ingredient
- liquid bleach
- pair of rubber or plastic kitchen gloves

You may be familiar with one group of microorganisms called *bacteria*. Some bacteria cause disease in humans, but most pose no health threat to humans. In fact, some types of bacteria are very beneficial. One such type lives in your intestines. These bacteria make vitamin K, something you need to remain healthy.

However, some of the bacteria that enter your body can cause disease. These bacteria may cause tooth decay, ulcers, and even life-threatening diseases such as food poisoning or meningitis. Fortunately, the human body has several ways of killing bacteria before they do any damage. The first line of defense is the skin. It prevents bacteria from entering the body in the first place.

Washing with soap and water keeps the skin clean and helps to wash away bacteria and other disease-causing microorganisms. Some liquid soaps contain an ingredient that kills bacteria. These soaps often include the word *antibacterial* on their labels. You can test how well these soaps kill bacteria with this experiment.

Thoroughly clean two small glass jars with liquid soap and water. Be sure to rinse the jars thoroughly with running water. Label one jar A, the other B. Half fill both jars with chicken broth. Add 1 teaspoon of sugar to each jar. Stir the broth until the sugar dissolves. The chicken broth and sugar will provide the nutrients that bacteria need to grow and multiply.

Add 1 teaspoon of liquid soap to the jar labeled A and stir gently. Place both jars in a spot where they are exposed to the air. Bacteria in the air will fall into the open jars. If these bacteria start to grow and multiply, you will notice that the broth turns cloudy, as shown in Figure 21. Of course, if the liquid soap is effective, the broth should remain clear—or at least stay clear longer than the broth that has no liquid soap. Design an experiment to determine how much soap is needed to slow or prevent the growth of bacteria. You can either add more soap at

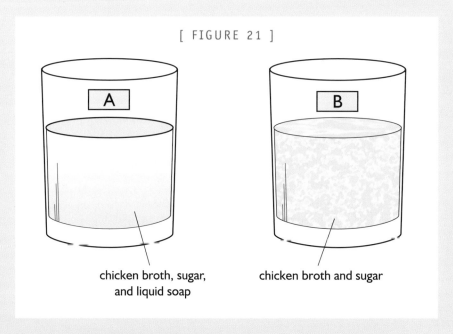

[FIGURE 21]

A

B

chicken broth, sugar, and liquid soap

chicken broth and sugar

The cloudiness of the broth on the right is due to the growth of bacteria. These bacteria can even form solid clumps over time.

the beginning or add a little each day as your experiment progresses. Keep a record in your notebook.

If bacteria grow in the broth, be sure that you do not touch the broth. Also be sure that none of the broth spills. The bacteria growing in the broth may be capable of causing disease. When you are finished with your broth, put on a pair of rubber or plastic kitchen gloves. **Under adult supervision**, fill each jar with liquid bleach. Allow the jars to remain undisturbed for 24 hours. The bleach will kill the bacteria. Once the bacteria have been killed, you can pour the contents down a drain and flush thoroughly with running water. Rinse the jars with running water. Wash them thoroughly with soap and warm water before using them to store any food or liquids.

Science Fair Project Idea

Antibacterial household products that kill bacteria are not limited to hand soaps. Other products include hand lotions, dishwashing detergents, sponges, kitchen cutting boards, plastic wrap for foods, pillows, sheets, mattress pads, socks, athletic shoes, toothpastes, and even toys. The active ingredient in most of these products is an antibacterial chemical called triclosan. Triclosan is even added to the metal used to make small kitchen appliances such as toasters and mixers.

(continued on next page)

(continued from previous page)

It would seem that bacteria do not stand a chance of surviving in a household equipped with all these products. In fact, using these products would seem to guarantee a germ-free household. However, scientists have expressed a serious concern about the increasing number of household products that contain an antibacterial ingredient. One concern is that these products destroy good bacteria as well as those that cause disease. Another concern is that these products cannot kill all the harmful bacteria. Those that survive may produce *immune* strains that will pose a serious threat to human health in the near future.

Using the Internet, research and make a list of all the household products that contain an antibacterial ingredient. How many of these products do you have in your home? With the help of a teacher or **other adult**, design an experiment that tests whether such a product actually reduces the number of bacteria. You can base your design on Experiment 5.5. For example, brush your teeth first thing in the morning with a toothpaste that does not contain an antibacterial ingredient. Then wipe your teeth with a cotton swab. Next, stir the swab in chicken broth and sugar. Cover the liquid with foil and check to see if bacteria grow. Do the same the following morning with toothpaste that contains an antibacterial ingredient. Does brushing with this toothpaste get rid of more bacteria?

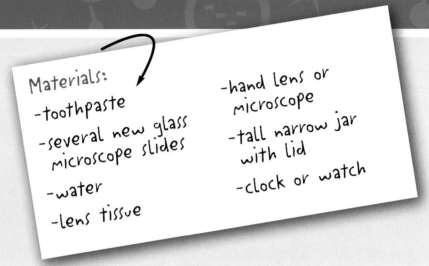

Materials:
- toothpaste
- several new glass microscope slides
- water
- lens tissue
- hand lens or microscope
- tall narrow jar with lid
- clock or watch

With the increased amount of sugars and soft foods in our diets, the incidence of tooth decay has risen sharply in many areas of the world. As a result, tooth decay has become the most common disease in the world. Nearly everyone will at some point in his or her life get tooth decay. This situation would be much worse if it were not for toothpaste.

Tooth decay is caused by a sticky substance called *plaque*. Plaque develops when bacteria in the mouth break down sugars on your teeth. The bacteria change the sugars into plaque, which destroys the enamel surface of teeth. As this enamel layer is gradually destroyed, a cavity forms. Brushing with toothpaste removes plaque found on the surface of teeth. To remove plaque, a toothpaste must be able to cause *abrasion*. Abrasion is simply the ability to remove something by rubbing it. The more abrasion a toothpaste can cause, the better it is at removing plaque. However, too much abrasion can damage tooth enamel.

Place a small dab of toothpaste on a new, clean glass microscope slide. Place another new slide on top. Gently rub the two slides back and forth 50 times. Remove the top slide and wash it with running water. Dry the slide with lens tissue. Examine the slide under a microscope or with a hand lens. If there are only a few scratches on the slide, then rate the abrasive action of the toothpaste as light. If the slide has many scratches, then rate it as heavy. Anything in between would be rated as moderate abrasive action. It will be easier to tell the difference between light, moderate, and heavy abrasion if you carry out this experiment with different brands of toothpaste. Just be sure to treat each brand in exactly the same way so that you have only one independent variable, the brand.

Toothpastes also contain a soap to clean the teeth. You can check the cleansing action of a toothpaste by placing some in a tall narrow jar. Use an amount equal to what you would put on a toothbrush. Half fill the jar with water. Put the lid on the jar and shake vigorously for one minute. A toothpaste that cleans well will foam easily. Repeat this procedure to check different toothpaste brands for their cleansing action.

Science Fair Project Ideas

- The ingredient in some toothpastes that provides the abrasive action is calcium carbonate. The soap in toothpaste is usually sodium lauryl sulfate. You may not have heard of either of these ingredients, but you probably have heard of one of the other ingredients in toothpaste: fluoride. Fluoride hardens the enamel surface of teeth, so it helps prevent tooth decay. But fluoride in toothpaste can pose a serious problem for children under the age of six, who can develop a condition known as fluorosis. Once fluorosis occurs, it will not go away. Check the Internet for information on fluorosis. Find out why young children are most likely to develop it. Also check how the Food and Drug Administration (FDA) and the American Dental Association (ADA) have addressed this problem. Finally, take a close look at the label on a package of toothpaste. What warning does it provide for children under the age of six? (continued on next page)

(continued from previous page)

- Locate information on "natural" toothpastes. As part of your project, make your own fluoride-free toothpaste and check its abrasive and cleansing actions. You can locate recipes for making toothpaste on the Internet. One simple recipe calls for mixing three parts bicarbonate of soda with one part salt. Add 3 teaspoons of glycerin for every 1/4 cup of this mixture. Add enough water to make a thick paste. Add a few drops of peppermint oil for taste. Mix well and start brushing!

Materials:
- shampoo (at least 2 different brands)
- measuring cup
- measuring teaspoon
- large bowl
- large spoon
- tall, narrow glass jar with lid
- ruler
- India ink
- eyedropper
- tall, narrow glass container (bud vase works well)
- small marble or tiny steel ball bearing
- stopwatch, or clock or watch with second hand

All shampoos contain an ingredient that cleans hair by allowing the oils and grease to mix with water. This ingredient is actually a *detergent*, and it causes the natural oil in hair, known as *sebum*, to mix with water so that the dirt can be washed away. Because all shampoos contain a detergent, all brands can get hair clean. If that is the case, can one brand of shampoo be any better than another? Carry out this experiment with at least two different shampoo brands to find the answer. If possible, compare an expensive brand to an inexpensive brand.

Prepare a one percent solution of each brand of shampoo. To do this, dilute 1 teaspoon of the shampoo in 2 cups of water in a large bowl. Use a large spoon to mix the shampoo gently to avoid producing soap bubbles. Pour ¼ cup of the diluted shampoo into a tall, narrow glass jar. To avoid producing any foam, pour the diluted shampoo down the inner side of the jar.

Screw the lid on the jar. Measure the height of the shampoo. Shake the jar vigorously ten times. Measure the height of the foam. A good shampoo will produce at least twice its volume in foam when shaken ten times. Thus, the height of the foam should be twice that of the shampoo. Repeat this procedure three times and average the results. Each time, rinse the jar and use fresh solution.

Rinse out the jar. Pour another ¼ cup of diluted shampoo into the jar. Add 1 drop of India ink, put the lid on the jar, and shake ten times. Look to see if the India ink has spread out in the liquid, in the foam, or both. Good shampoos will cause solids, such as dirt and India ink, to spread out in the liquid. That way the dirt can be washed away with water. Dirt and grease trapped in the foam are more difficult to wash

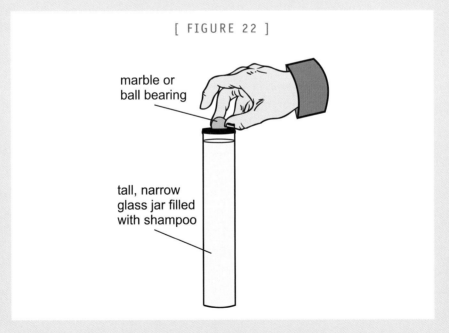

[FIGURE 22]

marble or
ball bearing

tall, narrow
glass jar filled
with shampoo

Gently place a ball bearing or small marble on the surface. Time how long it takes for it to fall to the bottom.

away with water. Repeat this procedure three times and average the results.

The "body" of a shampoo is known as its *viscosity*. The higher the viscosity, the thicker or more concentrated the shampoo. To determine the viscosity of a shampoo, fill a tall, narrow, glass container with undiluted shampoo. Determine the time it takes for a small marble or tiny ball bearing to fall to the bottom of the glass container, as shown in Figure 22. The greater the viscosity of the shampoo, the longer it will take for the object to fall to the bottom. The more concentrated the shampoo, the less you may need to clean your hair. Repeat this procedure three times and average the results.

Compare your results for the two shampoo brands you tested for their ability to foam, their ability to wash away dirt, and their viscosity. Make a table similar to Table 7 and summarize your findings. Is there any difference between shampoo brands? When you are finished with the experiment, pour any unused shampoo back into the original bottle.

Based on your data, which shampoo would you buy?

TABLE 7.

Average Test Results for Shampoo's Foaming Ability, Cleaning Ability, and Viscosity

Shampoo brand	Foaming ability	Cleaning ability	Viscosity
Brand 1	3 times height of liquid	Ink in liquid	3.5 seconds
Brand 2	Same height as liquid	Ink in foam	1.5 seconds

FURTHER READING

BOOKS

Bochinski, Julianne Blair. *The Complete Workbook for Science Fair Projects.* Hoboken, N.J.: John Wiley and Sons, Inc., 2004.

Moorman, Thomas. *How to Make Your Science Project Scientific.* Revised Edition. New York: John Wiley & Sons, Inc., 2002.

Rogers, Kirsteen. *The Usborne Internet-Linked Library of Science: Human Body.* London, England: Usborne Publishing Ltd., 2001.

Shanley, Ellen and Colleen Thompson. *Fueling the Teen Machine.* Palo Alto, Calif.: Bull Publishing Co., 2001.

Smolin, Lori A. and Mary B Grosvenor. *Nutrition and Weight Management.* Philadelphia: Chelsea House Publishers, 2005.

Viegas, Jennifer. *The Heart: Learning How Our Blood Circulates.* New York: The Rosen Publishing Group, Inc., 2002.

INTERNET ADDRESSES

Centers for Disease Control and Prevention. *Bam! Body and Mind.* 2008.
http://www.bam.gov

Nemours Foundation. *Kids Health: For Kids.* 1995–2008.
http://www.kidshealth.org

United States Department of Agriculture. *MyPyramid.gov.* 2008.
http://www.mypyramid.gov/

INDEX

INDEX

metabolic rate
    basal, 47–50
    defined, 47
    food and, 51
    thyroid hormone and, 48
    total, 51–54
metabolism, 47
microorganisms, disease and, 110–112, 116
milk, density by type, 81–84
minimal erythmal dose (MED), 105–106
MyPyramid, 79–80

N

niacin, 98
nutritional value assessment, 58, 85. *See also* food labels.

O

obesity, 45, 69–71
oils, 80
olestra (Olean), 92
osteoporosis, 103
oxalic acid, 64

P

pellagra, 97–98
percent daily value, 59–61
personal hygiene products, 96, 110–125
perspiration, 35, 37
physical fitness defined, 14–15
pinch test, 78
plaque, 120
potato chips, history of, 87–89
pressure defined, 21
protein, 55, 68
pulse measurement, 16–18
pulse pressure, 21

R

radial artery, 16

S

safety, 9, 39
satiety, nervous regulation of, 70
science fairs, 7–9
scientific method, 10–11
scurvy, 96–97

Semmelweis, Ignaz, 111–112
shampoos, 123–125
soap
    antibacterial, 96, 116–119
    standard, 113–115
sphygmomanometers, 22
spirometers, 39
stethoscopes, 17
stress, 13–14
sugars, 80, 91, 93–94
sun exposure, vitamin D and, 66
sun protection factor (SPF), 105–106
sunscreens, 96, 105–108
supplemental air, 39, 41–42
systolic pressure, 21

T

temperature
    body (*See* body temperature)
    density and, 84
temporal artery, 17
thermometers, 24
thyroid hormone, metabolic rate and, 48
tidal air, 39–41
tooth decay, 120, 121
toothpaste, 120–122

U

ultraviolet (UV) radiation, 105

V

vegetables, 99
viscosity, determining, 125
vital capacity measurements, 39–43
vitamins
    A, 103
    B, 98, 102
    C (ascorbic acid), 98–102
    D, 66
    overview, 96–98, 102–103
volume conversions, 81–82

W

water density, 82–84
weight, 37, 69, 72

Z

zinc oxide, 108